To my cherished grandparents and great-grandparents. This was their time.

DELAWARE
IN WORLD WAR I

★

Brigadier General Kennard R. Wiggins Jr. (DE ANG Retired)

H
THE
History
PRESS

Published by The History Press
Charleston, SC 29403
www.historypress.net

Front cover, top, left: Armistice Day celebration. *Courtesy Library of Congress.*
Front cover, top, right: A self-portrait of Lieutenant Walter Willoughby Josephs with his bomber. *Courtesy Marjorie Vaughn.*
Front cover, bottom, left: A U.S. Shipping Board poster depicting a sailor, shipbuilder and soldier. *Courtesy Library of Congress.*
Front cover, bottom, right: Women marching in national suffrage demonstration in Washington, D.C., on May 9, 1914. *Courtesy Library of Congress.*
Back cover, top: The troopship *Leviathan* putting to sea with thousands of troops from Hoboken, New Jersey. *Courtesy Library of Congress.*
Back cover, inset: *Delaware Awake!* by Ethel Pennewill Brown, 1918. *Courtesy University Museums, University of Delaware, Gift of Women's Liberty Loan Committee, 1918.*

First published 2015

ISBN 978.1.54021.404.1

Library of Congress Control Number: 2015942273

CONTENTS

PREFACE

My primary personal interest has been to chronicle the historical progress of the Delaware National Guard, leading me to write a history of the Fifty-ninth Pioneer Infantry Regiment, which was largely composed of the boys from Delaware who fought in France during the Great War. However, their story has a large prelude—most of these same fellows were deployed to the Mexican border in 1916 to pursue Pancho Villa following his depredations in the Southwest United States. I found these young men, their stories and the world events that shaped them to be a fascinating study.

I liked their rural "cowboy" heritage on the border, and their willingness to go overseas to an exotic foreign land to defend the United States. They straddled a point in history between horses and mechanized weapons, between the quaint rural customs of the nineteenth century and the rush of events toward an industrial society driven by the war. These were interesting times, and I began to broaden my brush and collect, as a sort of byproduct, assorted stories and facts about World War I in general. The upcoming centennial celebrations of the Great War also tended to lend focus to my research.

In so doing, I studied the history of one of America's dreadnoughts, the USS *Delaware*; the fortifications erected along the Delaware estuary; the industrial growth in the state; and the many individual stories of men and women who fought or contributed in some way to the effort to gain victory over the Central powers. I found dramatic stories of romance, explosions, piracy, national health issues, submarines, espionage, shortages, tribulations, sacrifice and more. I uncovered more and more voices through diaries, letters and newspaper articles.

As it happens, there are very few titles dedicated to Delaware history during this time period. One can find numerous books dedicated to the Civil War and to World War II for Delaware. The only previous Delaware-themed World War I title, of which I am aware, is Francis Ianni's *World War One Remembered*.

So I have widened my scope and taken a rather broad view in time and geography in compiling this book. It is the story of a war and its effect on Delawareans. However, it occasionally spills over a few borders and outside the normal chronology in telling this story of the Delaware people struggling to come to terms with a global war in a new century. It also wanders a little outside the normal bounds of military history to provide the context needed to understand this time and this place. My hope and aim is to provide the reader with an improved sense of what daily life was like in wartime Delaware during these formative years. I hope you will be transported to an interesting time in a very lively place.

ACKNOWLEDGEMENTS

The author would like to acknowledge the generous help he received from the following individuals, without whose help this project would have been impossible:

My commissioning editor, Banks Smither, for his firm hand on the tiller and keeping this book on a steady course to completion, and my production editor, Katie Stitely, for burnishing and polishing the final product.

My wife, Elizabeth, for her enduring support and her candid comments as the writing progressed.

Lieutenant General William Duncan, MD, for contributing his knowledge of Delaware military history and offering critical commentary.

Norma Jean Fowler, who was so helpful in the Laurel, Delaware Library special collections department.

Ed Richi and Dr. Constance Cooper of the Delaware Historical Society, who have been perennially helpful.

The helpful staff at the Delaware Public Archives.

Rebecca Melvin of the University of Delaware Library Special Collections Department.

"Missy" Vaughn, who introduced me to her family of veterans.

Joan Elliott Phillips and Kaesey McCormick, for reading my manuscript.

Dr. Janis A. Tomlinson, director of the University of Delaware Museum.

William H.J. Manthorpe Jr., for his generosity in sharing his resources regarding the maritime history of this period.

ACKNOWLEDGEMENTS

Arlene Marcley of the Shoeless Joe Jackson Museum, Greenville, South Carolina.

Marie Ferguson and Dick Berl, for sharing their father's memorabilia.

Kevin Martin of the Hagley Museum Library.

INTRODUCTION

T he Delaware General Assembly passed a resolution in March 1915 in reaction to the deepening conflict in Europe. The assembly resolved:

That we deeply deplore the world tragedy which is taking place in Europe. That we request President Woodrow Wilson to proffer the belligerents at such time as shall deem proper the good offices of the American government in the cause of peace, believing that his record and reputation single him out as preeminently qualified for so momentous a task.

In some respects, the resolution was a sort of mandatory nod to the events unfolding overseas, which were of no direct importance to the bystanders in the West, who could observe and comment from the high moral ground. Yet this first modest pronouncement was a small harbinger of the many steps to come that led to the full involvement of the United States and Delaware in a global war never before experienced.

Delaware is the second-smallest state in the nation but has always punched far above its weight. It lies near the halfway point of the Eastern Seaboard, offering a central strategic location for commerce. More importantly, it borders the Delaware Bay and River estuary and guards the mouth of an important manufacturing and cultural center on its upstream tributaries. During World War I, the Delaware estuary was an artery for locomotives, rifles, ammunition, black powder, chemicals, petroleum products, airplanes, shipbuilding and more to support the war effort. Illustrator Howard Pyle

Delaware Awake! by Ethel Pennewill Brown, 1918. A poster for the sale of war bonds whose iconography includes many Delaware state symbols. *Courtesy University Museums, University of Delaware, Gift of Women's Liberty Loan Committee, 1918.*

described the state in 1879 as a place that has the "vim and progress of modern utilitarianism" but said that the lower counties were "indolence peculiar to southern life." Yet the lower counties also made a huge contribution to the war effort, thanks to downstate agricultural productivity.

A big impact of the Great War was economic. Although the conflict was relatively short in terms of American involvement (about nineteen months), the war lasted for more than four years altogether. War materiel orders from the combatants stimulated the Delaware economy.

Delaware was economically involved in the war long before it was formally declared by the United States. The war had been raging in Europe for over two and a half years before the United States formally entered the conflict. The munitions and armament manufacturers in Delaware had already begun to expand and export to the belligerent parties. Shipbuilders had already made plans to support the effort before the actual declaration of war in April 1917. As the United States entered the war, Delaware shipyards and powder mills were operating at near capacity. Prior to American entry into the war, individual volunteers had already enlisted in the British or Canadian forces.

Approximately 10,000 Delawareans entered the armed forces, but many of them were called up too late to participate in the fighting. According to the U.S. Department of Veterans Affairs, approximately 9,000 men from Delaware served in the armed forces overseas during the war in the army, navy and Marine Corps. This represented about 11.8 percent of the male population over eighteen years of age. Of that number, 43 Delawareans were killed in action, and 188 were wounded. Many more died in the flu epidemic engulfing the world. Total Delaware military fatalities at the end of the war numbered 270, including those lost to disease.

Delaware began to awaken to a new, larger reality. This tiny state was now connected intimately with a much wider world that was in roiling turmoil. The result was that Delaware made radical changes in its society, commerce and thinking about its place in the world.

A DARKENING SKY

A Prelude to War:
A Sketch of Prewar Delaware

In 1914, Delaware was a divided state. It had a bustling industrial north, concentrated near Wilmington, and an agrarian south. Agriculture remained the dominant factor in the state economy. The Great War would be a time of accelerating change for the entire state; technology would drive change in both industry and agriculture. Delaware's population in 1910 was 202,322. It grew to 223,003 by 1920. Almost all of that growth was in the urban north.

There were 10,836 farms listed in the 1910 Delaware census, with an average size of ninety-six acres. About 40 percent of farmers were tenant farmers. Mostly, they still used animal power because the census listed thirty-one thousand horses and six thousand mules. After 1910, there was a shift forward from growing staples, such as wheat and corn, to more perishable table products like tomatoes, peas, beans, potatoes, melons, asparagus and cucumbers.

Improved truck farming methods, mechanized farming and transportation infrastructure fostered this change, allowing produce to get to the market quicker and with wider distribution. Dairy production also increased, as well as the farming of strawberries, apples and peaches. The U.S. Department of Agriculture published a soil survey describing Kent County's rural lifestyle: "The County is well equipped with wagon roads, which are kept in

Packing berries in a field near Harrington, Delaware. *Courtesy Delaware Historical Society.*

moderately good condition. A few of the farmers have telephone service…a few farmers are using tractors and many own automobiles."

In a memoir, Walter M. Deputy described life around Milford, Delaware, as a ten-year-old boy just before the war. His description offers a glimpse of how varied and enterprising life in rural Delaware was at that time.

My first recollection of my father was as a millwright in a cannery in Milford, and a short stint in a shipyard in Milford. In those days we had a big garden and Pop and a neighbor would net fish in the Mispillion River, bringing in shad, herring, and trout in various seasons. Some of these fish were pickled in barrels for winter use. Of course we had a horse, buggy, and buckboard. Pop would go into the woods with a neighbor and cut wood for the cook stove and heat it in the winter. Around Thanksgiving Pop and a neighbor would collect holly and berries and willow branches for wreath frames. The women would make holly wreathes and send them to Wilmington and Philadelphia markets.

In the late fall there was hog killing. This meant building gallows, heating the large steel pots for scalding, cleaning entrails for stuffing sausage, making scrapple, salting hams and flitch or side belly. Sometimes we made wet fires in the smoke house using hickory and sassafras wood for hams and bacon. Usually we would bring pork, sausage and scrapple home. Other

Cutting hay near Wilmington, Delaware, at the turn of the century. *Courtesy Delaware Historical Society.*

times we would go to wheat threshings and bring wheat, corn or buckwheat to the mill on the way home and take flour, cornmeal, and buckwheat for hot cakes with us.

Grandpop and Grandma used to raise sugar cane. They had a mill that produced cane syrup. They would boil it in big outside pots making what they called "black strap molasses." It was used for sugar for coffee, cakes etc. As you can see very little money was exchanged except for buying kerosene for the lamps and such items as coffee, salt, and $6.00 per month for rent, clothing and all. They used to trade eggs for groceries, gunpowder, and other necessary items.

They spent a lot of time around the water, trapping, catching Diamondback Terrapin, snapping turtles and shipping them in barrels to Philadelphia. They also tonged for oysters, dug clams and caught crabs for commercial shipment to the cities. They hauled large seines or nets in the bay for fish, cut marsh hay which was used for packing in those days. Wheat and corn was also raised and was sold on shares with the owner. Some of the grain was taken to Waple's Mill for milling.

Grandpa specialized in raising watermelons, which were taken to Frederica by mule and wagon. These were loaded on boats and shipped to Philadelphia. I was fortunate enough to have made the trip with Grandpop, staying on the boat while Grandpop bartered on the wharf selling his

A Brosius and Smedley delivery truck picking up a load of supplies at the Baltimore and Ohio Railroad Depot in Wilmington, Delaware. *Courtesy Delaware Historical Society.*

watermelons. I was about ten years old and it was probably my greatest thrill. I saw my first street car, high buildings, paved streets with lights and lots of different people.

At the time, most bread (70 percent) was baked at home on a wood-fired stove, unless one lived in the city, where gas was available. The urban north was far different. Wilmington, the principal city, had a population of 87,411 in 1910, which swelled to 110,168 by 1920. Electricity had come to the cities, and electrical lighting was becoming the norm. The DuPont Powder Company was a national corporation, headquartered in Wilmington, with mills along the nearby Brandywine River. There were thriving shipbuilding companies—as well as tanneries, railroad coach builders, paper making, cotton weaving, iron and steel foundries and vulcanized fiber manufacturers—along the Christina River waterfront.

Wilmington was served by five steam railroads, three horse-car lines, an electric trolley line and steamboats. At one time, Wilmington was served

The DuPont Building at Eleventh and Market Streets in Wilmington, circa 1914. *Courtesy Delaware Historical Society.*

by nine newspapers, two theaters and thirty-three hotels. There were dozens of restaurants and scores of saloons to match the building boom in the city. Schools, hospitals and churches multiplied to match the growth in population.

The signs of prosperity seemed to be everywhere. The year before the Great War in Europe, the Women's College was founded at Newark, as well as Delaware College, later called the University of Delaware. The Hotel DuPont and Playhouse were opened in the new DuPont Building. The Wilson Line ferry began service between Wilmington and Pennsville, New Jersey. The New Castle County Courthouse on Rodney Square was completed in 1917. Hospitals were opened in Milford and Lewes. Electrical power was extended to small towns downstate, such as Blades, Greenwood and Bethel.

This was the age of Progressivism. In reaction to the extremes of rapid industrialization and urbanization, America was experiencing social turmoil. Large corporations were combining into even more powerful monopolies and trusts, which seemed to be beyond the reach of law. Governments ruled by machine politics, and business interests corrupted entrenched politicians. Consumers had no recourse against substandard goods and services, and workers had no protection against exploitation.

Crusading journalists focused the public's attention and anger on these inequities. Their aim was to protect fair competition and tame the extremes of corporate trusts. New political leaders arose who tackled these new challenges and infused public life with optimism. There were other involved leaders at all levels of government and in civic associations outside of government. Their effective blend of idealism and realism created some of the most important and useful reforms in American history. By January 24, 1914, the popular magazine *Collier's* claimed that the previous ten years of the Progressive era was "the period of the greatest ethical advance made by this nation in any decade." These reforms had been a bipartisan effort, starting in the 1890s and concluding in the 1920s. The national political leaders included Theodore Roosevelt, Robert M. La Follette Sr. and Charles Evans Hughes on the Republican side and William Jennings Bryan, Woodrow Wilson and Al Smith on the Democratic side. In 1915, child labor laws passed, and Delaware created a state labor commission. However, not all the social problems were solved. As elsewhere, harsh Jim Crow policies were in effect, and racial segregation ruled. The struggle between capital and labor continued.

Two other social issues dominated the political landscape during the second decade of the new century. Progressivism fed the twin movements of women's suffrage and Prohibition. Many Progressives supported Prohibition in order to destroy the political power of local political bosses, who were often based in saloons. The National Temperance Council was founded in 1913 to promote the temperance movement.

"Last call." Interior of a crowded bar moments before midnight on June 30, 1919, when wartime prohibition went into effect. *Courtesy Library of Congress.*

At the same time, women's suffrage was promoted to bring the vote to women. In 1913, onlookers attacked a suffragette march in Washington, D.C., while police stood by. This struggle continued throughout the war years and beyond, until the passage of the Nineteenth Amendment in 1920.

Culturally, this was the age of the famous Armory Show in New York City, featuring Marcel Duchamp's *Nude Descending a Staircase*, described by one critic as "an explosion in a shingle factory." The show displayed the works of artists who became some of the most influential painters of the early twentieth century. Jim Thorpe, arguably the greatest all-round American athlete, was compelled to relinquish his 1912 Olympic medals for having briefly played semi-pro baseball. After arriving in Hollywood, Cecil B. DeMille began shooting the first feature-length film made there. Edgar Rice Burroughs published *Tarzan of the Apes*.

In Delaware, the Brandywine School was established by nationally known illustrator Howard Pyle, spawning the Wyeth dynasty, Frank Schoonover, Gail

A Boy Scout troop master and his troop. *Courtesy Delaware Historical Society.*

Hoskins and others. The Wilmington Society of Fine Arts was incorporated in 1912. In 1916, the Boy Scouts movement was established in Delaware.

The U.S. Navy completed "Plan Black," meant for a war with Germany, envisioning an attempt to invade the Caribbean. In 1913, the U.S. Navy used aircraft on maneuvers for the first time, off Cuba. America had spent less than $0.5 million on military aviation since 1908, only one-fiftieth the amount that France or Germany had. This was not surprising, as the United States was a neutral nation at peace, insulated by two oceans. Spending on weapons and armies was a low priority. All this began to change as Europe erupted into war in August 1914.

It is not my place here to describe the detailed causes of this world war. However, to provide context, a few key events will be detailed. A long and relatively peaceful period of European history ended when a series of alliances between the Central powers (Germany and Austria-Hungary) declared war on the Allied powers (France, Russia and, later, the United Kingdom, in response to the assassination of an heir to the Austrian throne in Sarajevo, Bosnia, in June 1914). The linking treaties and pacts caused a cascade of events that resulted in the German invasion of Russia, Luxembourg, Belgium and France.

The German Hamburg liner *Kronprinzessin Cecilie. Courtesy U.S. Naval Historical Center.*

The Central powers were later joined by Bulgaria and Turkey. The Allies were later joined by Italy, Japan, China and Belgium.

The unforeseen result of this Balkan squabble was a globe-spanning conflict that eventually included the United States, in 1917. Americans declared neutrality and did their best to keep this war on the other side of the ocean. Public opinion was not sympathetic to American involvement. Nevertheless, the war could not be ignored and began, by degrees, to have an impact here at home, despite America's best intentions.

An example of the immediate impact of the conflict was the adventure that Delaware's governor had on the very first day of declared war.

GOVERNOR MILLER IMPACTED AT SEA, AUGUST 1914

Among the very first and most prominent Delaware citizens to be affected by the outbreak of war in Europe was Delaware governor Charles Miller. In the summer of 1914, Miller and his wife took a cruise to Europe for a holiday in Russia. They booked passage on the North German Lloyd liner *Kronprinzessin Cecilie.*

Their adventure began when England declared war on Germany. The *Cecilie* instantly became an enemy combatant in hostile waters, just two days away from England.

There is a legend that the *Cecilie* was in the English Channel under chase by the Royal Navy. According to the story, Governor Miller and other passengers on the largely North American passenger list were able to successfully talk the captain into turning the ship toward Falmouth Harbor and turning himself and his vessel over to the English authorities. For his troubles, the English detained the governor for about a month until the matter was sorted out. He returned to Delaware as the first local hero of the European war. It is uncertain how this story gained credence, but the actual events verified by naval records follow.

On its way from New York City to Bremen, Germany, with more than $10 million in gold and silver packed in its hold, the *Cecilie* carried hundreds of Americans and Europeans on holiday or business. On August 4, when England declared war on Germany, two days out from the English coast, Captain Charles Polack turned the ship around and headed back to the United States in search of a neutral port. Passengers knew about the change in direction only after they noticed "the position of the moon had unaccountably shifted to the port side of the ship."

The *Bangor Daily Commercial*'s front page told the story in a multi-tiered headline: "*Kronprinzessin Cecilie* a Refugee at Bar Harbor: North German Lloyd Liner With $10,600,000 in treasure, 1500 Passengers, Sought All Over the North Atlantic, Escapes British Cruisers and With Lights Masked Flees Across the Ocean to Maine Coast."

The 685-foot *Cecilie* had dropped anchor early that morning after a four-day run across the fog-shrouded ocean. Captain Charles Polack had picked up wireless signals indicating French and British warships knew of his ship's whereabouts and valuable cargo.

There were several reasons for choosing Bar Harbor. Among the passengers was C. Ledyard Blair, whose family owned a "cottage" at Bar Harbor. An experienced yachtsman, Blair piloted the ship to the harbor. The captain publicly thanked Blair through the Bangor newspapers the day they arrived.

Special Maine Central trains were outfitted in Bangor to take the *Cecilie*'s passengers back to New York. The city "was forcibly reminded that a great European war, to be perhaps the worst that the world has ever witnessed, is in progress," wrote a reporter for the *Bangor Daily News* on August 5.

Not everyone left Bar Harbor, however. Governor and Mrs. Charles Miller of Delaware gave up plans to visit Russia, deciding instead to spend some time at Bar Harbor. He would return to Delaware after a month and preside over the industrial build-up that would dominate the state's economy in the first years of World War I.

The *Cecilie* rapidly became a tourist attraction for the three months it was moored at Bar Harbor. Commandeered by the United States on February 3, 1917, the ship was transferred to the navy when America entered the war; it was renamed *Mount Vernon*. *Mount Vernon* departed New York for Brest on October 31, 1917, on its first crossing for the navy. It made nine successful voyages carrying doughboys to Europe during the war.

The *Kronprinzessin Cecilie* affair was a foretaste of what was to come. Bit by bit, the United States would be drawn into the global conflict.

DELAWARE REACTS TO THE HOSTILITIES IN EUROPE

Woodrow Wilson declared the United States a neutral country and attempted to steer clear of what was seen as a singularly European struggle. In 1916, he campaigned on a platform that included the slogan "He kept us out of the war."

The press published accounts of the horrors of the war. No one wanted any part of that conflict, and few imagined Delaware as a participant. Delaware was enjoying peace and prosperity. Governor Simon Penniwell, in his final message to the legislature in 1913, declared the future "never looked brighter." Respect for law and a feeling of patriotism seemed to be the pattern of life.

Despite the troubles in Europe, a more immediate threat on America's borders drew the attention of the nation in 1916.

DELAWARE NATIONAL GUARD DURING THE PUNITIVE EXPEDITION TO MEXICO, 1916–1917

When trouble broke out along the Mexican border in 1916, Delaware men were among the first to answer the call. A series of raids and depredations on American soil by the Mexican bandito Pancho Villa drew an armed response, led by U.S. Army general John J. Pershing. The national mood was one of "about time" after two years of fruitless negotiations. Initially, people felt that the National Guard was being used for political purposes in an election year; however, this changed to a feeling of patriotic pride after the raids on Columbus, New Mexico. A newly organized Delaware National

Members of Company D, Delaware National Guard. *Left to right*: First Sergeant Herman Ahlens, Captain Isaac Millis and Private L. Irving Handy. *Courtesy Delaware Historical Society.*

Guard was called for federal service on July 19, 1916, and mustered at the state rifle range in New Castle.

The men were then rushed through a brief and desultory medical examination. The naked men were weighed and measured for height and chest dimensions. A surgeon listened to the men's hearts and lungs, cracked their knees and checked for ruptures and diseases. The next doctor looked at their teeth and checked their vision. The entire process lasted about five minutes. A contemporary account commented on the pale, various fat and skinny ridiculous appearances of the men who were dressed only "in nature's garb." Very few were disqualified. Some of those considered unfit were shipped anyway and asked to sign a waiver of pension rights due to their previous disabilities!

The Delaware boys got their first taste of excitement on the way to Deming, New Mexico, during a five-day journey. As their troop train neared Sierra Blanca, Texas, stones were thrown at the train, and six gunshots broke windows on two of the cars. There were no injuries, and the train continued on, arriving in Deming on August 1 with 551 men. They received a grand welcome from the mayor and citizens.

On arrival in the Southwest, the men detrained and made camp, unfolding their cots and preparing to sleep out in the open under a wonderful southern sky. One soldier described it as being "in God's outdoors with only the sky as our canopy and ten million stars as our light." The men laid out their camp on a barren plateau the following day, measuring the distance for their company streets in perfect lines. Bathhouses and latrines were constructed, and water connections were established. Trenches were dug for drainage. The camp in Deming, New Mexico, was known as Camp Brooks, later renamed Camp Cody during World War I. It was only a few miles north of Columbus, which Pancho Villa had previously raided. The basic staples of life in the garrison were well provided for, but one correspondent commented on the difficulty and red tape required to fill in the gaps. There was bread but no butter, coffee without sugar and potatoes without salt. He quoted a little ditty of the time:

This is Second Lieutenant Harry B. Van Sciver of Company C. He would later serve as Delaware's selective service director during the 1940s. *Courtesy Delaware Military Heritage and Education Foundation.*

Sou-pee, sou-pee, sou-pee;
Without a single bean
Por-kee, por-kee, por-kee;
Without a strip of lean
Cof-fee, cof-fee, cof-fee;
without a drop of cream!

The army was short on blankets, too. Those who know the desert know that even a July night can be cold. There were shortages of cots, tents, pistols and more. Sanitation was a huge problem—there was a continual battle against flies and other vermin. Incinerators lined with brick and stone were constructed on every company street. Fires were maintained to dispose of refuse and dishwater. The incinerators were periodically dismantled, and crude oil was poured on the surrounding ground to destroy fly larvae. Every company was required to regularly police its site. Medical personnel examined the men daily. Each man was inoculated for typhoid on arrival

The bulletin board in Camp Brooks in Deming, New Mexico, with three unidentified soldiers. *Courtesy Marie Ferguson.*

at camp. In addition, there were regular foot inspections. Soldiers had to remove their shoes and socks for examination by company officers and surgeons. Clean socks and regular bathing were required. The payoff was a much-reduced level of disease compared to the experience during the Spanish-American War. The health of the men was probably better than it would have been at home. These were valuable lessons that would later be applied during the Great War.

The Young Men's Christian Association, or YMCA, provided remedies for the shortcomings of camp life. It had magazines, a phonograph, tables and stationery with which the boys could write home. It was a home away from home for the soldiers in their off-hours. They entertained themselves with card games and played baseball with a team led by John O'Daniel, a standout athlete.

Music was a big factor in the lives of the soldiers. At night, while marching along the company streets, or within the tents on a rainy day, there was always a song in the air. According to a correspondent:

There is nothing finer that soldiers can do. It uplifts the spirit of the camp and makes every one from the Colonel to the youngest rookie feel contented and secure. More than once I have heard the officers say, "When they are singing we know that everything is all right." Some of the companies sang songs that were elegant, others songs that were vulgar. The songs that companies sing serve as criteria of character by which you can not only judge the standard of the boys but even more the character of their officers.

A favorite song of the camp was:

I want a girl just like the girl that married dear old dad/She was a pearl, and the only girl that daddy ever had/A good, old-fashioned girl with heart so true, one who loves nobody else but you.

The men had a new version of the "Old Oaken Bucket," in which they lamented:

The old company tooth brush, the old company tooth brush, the old company tooth brush, that hung in the sink; first it was Borgmeier's, then it was Cheney's, then it was Frisbie's.

In December, a serious health problem developed. There was an outbreak of measles, leading to death by pneumonia. The Delaware regiment, the members of which were mostly from the city, experienced no fatalities, but other units in Deming were not so fortunate.

In his biennial report to Honorable Governor Charles R. Miller, dated December 31, 1916, Adjutant General I.P. Wickersham reported:

Two battalions of infantry, with the hospital detachment are now in Federal service at Deming, New Mexico, where they have been stationed since July 31 last (1916). In accordance with your verbal order of September 21, I proceeded to Deming, New Mexico, reaching there on October 1 and found the troops in excellent health, well supplied and equipped, camp site and sanitary conditions excellent. The troops were undergoing an intensive military training, which I am pleased to say was indicated by their appearance both physical and military. The troops have been on the border for five months and have performed their duty honestly and faithfully and without complaint, and it is hoped that they may be returned to their home stations in the near future...All officers and men were required to pass a rigid physical examination under the direction of a medical officer of the Army, and the necessary property and equipment was transferred to the property officers of the organization. The final muster into United States service

First Delaware Regiment officers and noncommissioned officers pose in camp with their Delaware sign. Major Warner Reed, commander of the First Delaware Infantry is third from the left in the second row. *Courtesy Delaware Military Heritage and Education Foundation.*

was completed on July 12, and the troops left Delaware for Deming, New Mexico on July 25, where they have been stationed ever since.

—Major J. Warner Reed

The two battalions of the First Delaware Infantry Regiment were, at different times, commanded by Major J. Warner Reed, Colonel H.L. Roberts and Major F.W. Cobbe. In his biennial report to Honorable Governor John G. Townsend, dated December 31, 1918, Adjutant General I.P. Wickersham reported:

The two battalions of Infantry, with Supply and Sanitation Detachments, which were called into the Federal Service in June 1916 for duty on the Mexican Border arrived home on February 8, 1917 for muster out. The first battalion was ordered to Wilmington; the second, with Supply and Sanitary Detachments, to Fort DuPont. The work of mustering out these troops was completed on February 15th, after which they resumed their State status. These troops were reviewed by the Governor upon their arrival at Wilmington and made a splendid showing. After the review, both officers and men were entertained at dinner at the Hotel DuPont by the General

A DARKENING SKY

Assembly, and in recognition of their services, each officer and man was presented with a medal provided by an act of the General Assembly.

On February 2, 1917, the First Delaware boarded trains for the journey home; their departure was accompanied by a noisy farewell from the citizens of Deming. The Delaware troops' service on the border, like that of the rest of the nation's National Guard, turned out to be more significant for its training value in preparation for the world war than for its actual accomplishments as an army in the field. Contemporary accounts of the deployment detailed the rigor of the training. Drilling was never relaxed. It was a daily occurrence, usually morning and afternoon. Bayonet drills were also emphasized because of the recent combat experience in the European war. The soldiers practiced fire distribution and firing discipline, as well as battle practice with combat problems and solutions, making use of the map and signals. These maneuvers were no make-believe endeavor. Under the tutelage of army officers, these citizen-soldiers were disciplined and trained under live fire conditions. The men were equipped with new Springfield rifles, and many soldiers experienced the deadly lethality of the machine gun for the first time in maneuvers. The men started the day with calisthenics immediately after roll call. There were endless daily hikes, which hardened the men and inured them to hardship.

The soldiers usually carried packs, rifles, bayonets, pistols and other equipment. The hikes would sometimes be up to twenty-five miles over two days in southwestern summer sunshine. Initially, the green civilians fell like flies, some requiring ambulances; but over time, they became conditioned to the rigors of the climate and terrain. They learned to hoard their water and conserve their strength. They lost flab and gained muscle, adding years to their lives. They developed into the best physical shape most of them had ever experienced. Their issued uniforms no longer fit their lean, hard frames. The Delaware soldiers had made a true transition from citizen to soldier during this demanding deployment.

Of the men who received their first military training in the ranks of the Delaware battalions, the most famous is Lieutenant General John W. (Iron Mike) O'Daniel, USA (retired), who was a private and later supply sergeant in Newark's Company E. Among the officers were two later adjutants general of Delaware, J.A. Ellison and William Berl Jr., and a future commander of the Delaware regiment, John P. LeFevre. Some of the officers who were to lead the 198th Coast Artillery in World War II had just started the climb up through the enlisted ranks, including Brigadier

General George J. Schulz and Lieutenant Colonels S.B.I. Duncan and Henry C. Ray. In 1957, Delaware's future state selective service director Brigadier General Harry B. Van Sciver was a second lieutenant in Company C. Another prominent guardsman deployed to the border was First Sergeant (Major, retired) Frederick L. Manion of Company F, one of the nation's outstanding marksman. He brought added laurels to the Delaware National Guard that year by placing second in the national championships with the high power rifle at Black Point Military Reservation in Jacksonville, Florida.

One legacy of the soldiers who went to the border was their name. The men were frequently covered with a heavy layer of southwestern dust and got the nickname "adobes." This was shortened to simply "dobies," which, some believe, is where the "doughboys" nickname of the First World War came from.

The Delaware men were glad to be home. Few of them realized that within two months they would be back in service, and this time, it would be the real thing.

2

FIRST SQUALL

"Delaware Always"

The call went out, that the State had need
For a War Defense, in word and deed
They rallied in haste as they were bid,
Just as Delaware always did.
   The good Blue Hen called to each chick,
They came at her clucking on double quick,
Ready to scratch for the mother still
Just as Delaware, always will.
   Forgetting all difference of mine and thine,
They gathered there by the Brandywine,
To stand by the guns, for the State's best good,
Just as Delaware, always would.
   From out of the good State's breadth and length,
The Diamond was there in its setting of strength,
Ready to do, with outstretched hands,
Just as Delaware, always stands.
   No partisan spirit was with them there,
But just the great heart of Delaware
In a brotherhood strong, that heart beat true,
As Delaware's heart will always do.
   Delaware down through the years to come,
Will follow the beat of the Fife and the Drum,
As she served of yore, she is serving still,
As Delaware always can, and always will.

AMERICA ENTERS THE WAR: MOBILIZATION

There were many factors that drove the United States to enter the war on the side of the Allied powers. Despite America's declared neutrality, the shocking invasion of neutral Belgium and the atrocities reported from that incursion reflected negatively on Germany from the start. President Wilson, in his 1914 neutrality speech, pleaded for Americans to "remain impartial in thought as well as in action." America might not have taken sides, but sympathy was mostly for the Allies.

That sympathy mirrored increasing hostility toward Germany, particularly after the unarmed passenger liner *Lusitania* was torpedoed without warning. There were 124 Americans among the 1,195 passengers lost. Germany attempted to make amends by placing certain restrictions on its own conduct at sea. America was a seafaring nation whose commerce was dependent on international trade. The global battle at sea negatively impacted America's ability to trade. The Allies blockaded the Central powers' ports, and Germany reacted with submarine warfare to inhibit Allied supply lines. America was drawn into this quagmire by degrees as it became a critical supplier for the combatants.

The Cunard liner *Lusitania* in a painting by Fred J. Hoertz. *Courtesy Library of Congress.*

The Central powers were slowly being strangled at home and suffering stalemates on the battlefield. In desperation, they unleashed unrestricted submarine warfare in 1917. To make matters worse, in early March 1917, an intercepted telegram called the "Zimmerman Note" indicated that Germany was plotting to bring Mexico into the war against America. This was the final straw, and on April 2, President Wilson asked for a declaration of war against Germany in order to "make the world safe for democracy," which was approved by Congress. To mark the occasion, a member

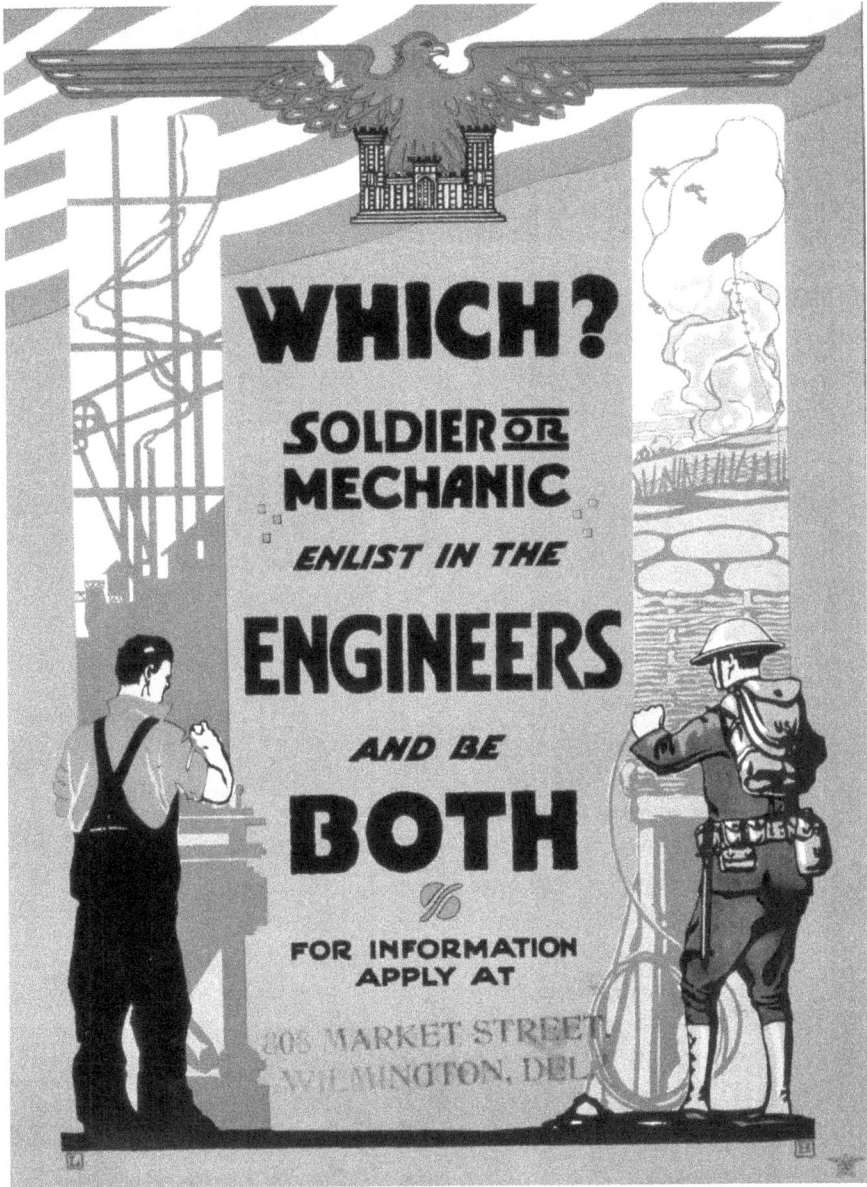

A recruiting poster in downtown Wilmington. *Courtesy Library of Congress.*

of the band from the Water Witch Fire Company went atop the fire tower at 1814 Gilpin Avenue in Wilmington and played "The Star-Spangled Banner" on his cornet.

The first and most important mobilization decision was the size of the army. When the United States entered the war, the army stood at 200,000, hardly enough to have a decisive impact in Europe. However, on May 18, 1917, a draft was imposed, and the number of enlisted men increased rapidly. Initially, the expectation was that the United States would mobilize an army of 1 million. The number, however, went much higher. Overall, some 4,791,172 Americans served in World War I. Delaware's contribution was about 10,000 men. Some 2,084,000 Americans reached France, and 1,390,000 saw active combat.

The nation and Delaware began to get ready to face this enormous challenge. Mobilization eventually impacted almost every citizen in one way or another. The *Philadelphia Inquirer* reported on September 4:

> *United States Officers, with horses and mules and two large team wagons, arrived on the Milford boat yesterday preparatory to surveying Sussex county in regard to the various bridges and roads which could be used for military purposes in case of an invasion. There are about twenty men in the party and the whole county is to be mapped off and defenses planned.*

The *Baltimore Sun* added on September 25:

> *Residents of Lewes and Sussex County are greatly interested in a report that the War Department intends to construct modern fortifications there, with long range rifles, to command the entrance to Delaware Bay as a further protection to League Island Navy Yard at Philadelphia, and the DuPont powder plant at Carney's Point. Two engineers of the War department have been in Lewes this week, going over land along the ocean and bay frontage there and considering advisability of sites for big fortifications. Modern defenses for Delaware Breakwater and the town may be embodied in the program for military preparedness to come before the next Congress. Should fortifications be erected to command the mouth of Delaware Bay it is expected they would be constructed at Cape May as well as Lewes, behind the Breakwater.*

When war was finally declared on Good Friday 1917, the Wilmington Park Board granted the use of the old town hall at 512 Market Street as storage for uniforms and quartermaster supplies to the National Guard. Schoolchildren flocked to the armory at Twelfth and Orange Streets, headquarters of the Delaware National Guard. They cheered the citizen-soldiers who grinned and waved back. It was a rainy day, and Easter weekend approached. Delaware had received a first quota for the army set at 2,259, and the state would go to work in earnest to fill its quota after the holiday. The lawmakers met in special session. The National Guard would be outfitted, and a state counsel of defense would be established.

Delaware College announced its intentions that a special unit might be organized for the army. Major Rolf J. Wysock, in his history of the Reserved Officer's Training Corps (ROTC) program at the University of Delaware, wrote:

> On July 1, 1918, the entire college plant was placed at the disposal of the War Department to be used in the training of mechanics for the national Army, and throughout the summer, classes had been busily working in the shops, taking courses in gas engines, electricity, radio, machine shop work, and bench wood work. Meantime Congress passed the bill creating the Students' Army Training Corps, an organization designed to prevent the destruction of the college threatened by the lowering of the draft age to 18, and to guarantee to the Army an adequate supply of officer material until the end of the war. In the fall the organization of the Delaware College Unit was begun. Many delays, chief amongst which was the epidemic of influenza, operated to prevent the smooth working of the new regime, but finally, in October, 215 students were regularly inducted into the United States Army for the unit. Academic instruction was carried on by the regular faculty. By June of 1918, 184 men (graduates and undergraduates) from the University of Delaware were on active duty in our Armed Forces. The unit was demobilized December 13, 1918 and the college was returned to civilian hands.

INDUSTRY GOES TO WAR

Military planning was only the obvious tip of the spear. An old military adage goes "strategy is for amateurs, logistics is for the professionals." Despite America's role as an emerging industrial powerhouse, its materiel contribution to the war effort was largely a case of too little too late. Americans fought with mostly French and British equipment. Their tanks and airplanes were of foreign manufacture. Nevertheless, Delaware was in the van of armament manufactures.

A U.S. munitions plant, 1916. *Courtesy Library of Congress.*

Chief among logistical concerns for the war was munitions. The DuPont Powder Company, headquartered in Wilmington, was well positioned to thrive during war. DuPont owned some forty gunpowder and explosives plants around the United States, putting it in a position to dominate its smaller competitors. On June 13, 1912, the District Court of the United States for Delaware had ordered that the DuPont Powder Company be broken up as part of the dissolution of the Powder Trust under the new Sherman Antitrust Act. The court decreed the formation of two new companies—Hercules Powder Company and Atlas Powder Company—that would receive some of DuPont's assets in order to become effective competitors.

Nevertheless, DuPont maintained its monopoly on the manufacture of gunpowder for the U.S. military—supposedly the object of the antitrust action in the first place. The company went on to make a fortune during the Great War by supplying the European Allies and later the U.S. Army with high-powered explosives for artillery shells.

Its very product, black powder, was a necessity for bullets, artillery and even the engineering aspects of modern warfare. It was also needed in inexhaustible quantities. DuPont was in a protected neutral country an ocean away from the hostilities. It quickly increased production to meet demand. Although powder for military uses composed only 5 percent of its business at the outset, DuPont was approached by the Allied powers to produce more. At first, the company was only able to supply 1 million pounds per month, but production soon grew to 1 million pounds per day. DuPont produced 40 percent of the explosives used by the Allied armed forces during the course of the Great War, amounting to 1.5 billion pounds. When the United States entered the war in 1917, DuPont provided a remarkable 100 percent of its explosives.

The company began exporting material to the combatants as early as 1915. It sold $25 million in powder and explosives in that first year. By 1918, the sales had increased to $319 million, totaling $1.245 billion in this five-year period ($28.289 billion in 2014 dollars). DuPont made $237 million in net profit, and its accumulated dividend over the war years yielded 458 percent of the stocks par value. Employment grew as well, from 5,300 employees in 1914 to 48,000 in 1918. In addition to munitions, DuPont produced coated fabrics for military clothing, paint for camouflage, adhesives for airplanes and material for gas mask eyepieces.

Other Delaware companies involved in war production were:

A. Jedal Company of Newark produced signal rockets, flares and smoke lights.

American Car and Foundry of Wilmington designed submarine chasers and produced pontoons and wooden pickets for bridge and river bank supports.

Pusey and Jones of Wilmington built cargo vessels, as well as castings and machinery for the caterpillar field gun.

Bethlehem Steel's New Castle Plant manufactured shells and munitions.

The Harlan Plant of Bethlehem Steel built commercial vessels.

Ball Grain Explosives of Wilmington produced 125,000 time fuses per day, as well as shrapnel shells and grenades.

Continental Fiber of Newark made Bakelite, a raw material used for gas mask goggles.

General Chemical Company's Delaware Valley Works—in Claymont, Delaware, and Marcus Hook, Pennsylvania—played an important supporting role in World War I, supplying Allied troops with critical ingredients for munitions and other supplies.

Vinyard Shipbuilding of Milford built tugs and submarine chasers for the navy.

Not all commerce was focused on the Delaware estuary. Southwest Delaware was also involved in trade in agricultural goods from the Nanticoke River to the Chesapeake Bay. There were noted shipbuilders in Bethel, Laurel and Seaford as well.

PIER, JERSEY CITY AFTER MUNITIONS EXPLOSION   3963.9

A pier in Jersey City after a munitions explosion, 1916. *Courtesy Library of Congress.*

FEARS OF SABOTAGE

With all these manufactured goods and war staples mostly being exported to the Allied powers, this bounty drew the attention of German saboteurs. Even before America's entry into the war, on July 30, 1916, a huge explosion rocked Jersey City at the "Black Tom" railway terminal. It was equivalent to a 5.4 magnitude earthquake, shattering windows in New York and felt as far away as Philadelphia. It was believed German saboteurs caused it. Another such explosion closer to home brought more suspicion.

Only days after the United States declared war on Germany, a huge explosion rocked the nearby Eddystone Pennsylvania Ammunition Plant, killing 133 people, mostly girls and young women hired to pierce fuses and fill shells with gunpowder for export to the Russian army. At first, many thought the explosion was an act of sabotage, as the United States had just entered the war only days before the explosion. Of the dead, fifty-five were never identified. The mystery of the explosion was never solved.

A smaller, less lethal explosion was recorded at the New Castle Bethlehem Steel Munitions Plant on December 12, 1917. It rocked the countryside and disrupted railroad and shipping traffic in the area.

German Scare

These incidents made the populace jittery and bred fear of German saboteurs. When war erupted in Europe, most Americans wanted no part of the Old World squabbles and were determined to stay out of it. Nevertheless, for many reasons, Americans began to feel sympathy for the French, British and Belgian Allies as a result of reported atrocities in neutral Belgium. They viewed the Germans as the ones who started the war, fueling a wave of anti-German sentiment at home. Further depredations brought America into the war, and Allied propaganda helped turn the Germans into dehumanized "others" to the American public.

German citizens were required to register with the federal government and carry their registration cards at all times. Some 2,048 German citizens were imprisoned beginning in 1917.

Delaware local schools ceased teaching German language courses, and books written in the German language were either banned or burned. Before the war, the German language had been America's second most widely used speaking language. Now, hysteria began to take hold. Recent German immigrants

1914 !

LES ASSASSINS !

A French anti-German propaganda poster from 1914 that reads "Les Assassins!" It depicts the Kaiser and his generals. *Courtesy Library of Congress.*

rushed to get their naturalization papers for fear they would be deported. Everything with German-associated names was changed. Hamburgers, which were named after the German city, were renamed Salisbury steaks. Frankfurters were renamed liberty sausages. Dachshunds became liberty dogs.

The Espionage Act of 1917 was passed to prevent spying but also contained a section that criminalized inciting or attempting to incite any mutiny, desertion or refusal of duty in the armed forces. Thousands of citizens were prosecuted on the authority of this act and the Sedition Act of 1918, which tightened restrictions even more. Conscientious objectors were punished as well, most of them Christian pacifist inductees.

The fledgling Mennonite community—which had settled near Greenwood, Delaware—fell under scrutiny. They were of mostly German descent, but their pacifist stance on the war brought even greater suspicion in the downstate community. For several years prior to the war, they had been granted the use of Carlisle Schoolhouse by the Greenwood School Board as a place of worship in return for providing firewood every week. One Saturday night, school board members informed the Mennonites that due to the intensity of the community feelings, the Mennonites were no longer welcome to use the school for worship services. The Mennonite men gave the place a good cleaning and returned the keys to the school board.

Dwight Warnick was a schoolboy at the time. He recalled:

I went to the school. All I remember is I was told we couldn't use it anymore. So we held services over at Val Bender's. We'd walk through the woods to meetings. I remember I was called a "damned old German" by another student in school. You were not popular if you spoke German in public. And I would have been less popular if they'd known my grandfather was a Hessian!

Laban Swartzentruber recounted that, as a high school student, he was asked to write a composition on why everybody should buy a liberty bond to supplement the war effort. Laban wrote, "Not everyone had to buy a bond, because in a free country that was not a requirement."

"The teacher became quite angry and denounced him before the class. She threw her books and stomped the floor and called the principal to the door." When the principal found out Laban had not been saluting the flag, she forced him to stand all day under the flag for the next couple of days. Laban dropped out of school for a short period after that until the matter was dropped.

Nevin Bender was a young man who had recently been ordained as a minister in the Mennonite community. He was drafted despite his status in the church. When he reported for training at Camp Meade, he told his commanding officer he could not participate in military training to carry a weapon or even wear a uniform. Designated as a conscious objector, he was assigned to clean toilets and warned to keep out of sight. When he was transferred to another unit, he was roughed up by the soldiers, who demanded to know why he did not wear a uniform. Bender was eventually permitted to work alternate service at dairy farms in Maryland and Pennsylvania.

After the war, he returned to Greenwood and became one of the leaders of his community. Despite the war and the influenza epidemic, the Mennonite community flourished and continues to thrive today.

PEACE MOVEMENT

The Mennonites were not the only pacifists. Led by British Quakers, the Friends' War Victims' Relief Committee and the Friends' Ambulance Unit began their efforts among noncombatants in 1914. These men and women were later joined by volunteers from the American Friends Service Committee, which was formed in 1917 when the United States entered the war. Together, the groups provided civilian relief in France, Belgium, Russia, Serbia, Austria and Poland and among the "alien enemies" in Great Britain. In 1919, Quakers extended their efforts to include a program to feed children in war-ravaged Germany.

The American Friends Service Committee (AFSC) was founded in 1917 during World War I to give young conscientious objectors ways to serve without joining the military or taking lives. They drove ambulances, ministered to the wounded and stayed on in Europe after the armistice to rebuild war-ravaged communities.

These various peaceful initiatives were but an eddy against a surging tide of national mobilization that included conscription and the activation of the National Guard.

An American field service poster created by Josef P. Nuyttens, 1917. *Courtesy Library of Congress.*

DELAWARE NATIONAL GUARD MOBILIZES

As international tensions arose, America went on the alert. War fever was growing, and even before hostilities were declared, national conscription was forwarded as a means to meet the threat and included in the Selective Service Act of 1917. National Guard units that had not yet completely mustered out from their Mexican border service were recalled to active duty. Among them was the First Delaware Infantry Regiment.

On March 25, 1917, only six weeks after they had returned from service on the Mexican border, the men of the First Battalion, First Delaware Infantry Regiment, were once again called into federal service. Led by Colonel J. Warner Reed, they were ordered to defend vital utility and communications points in Delaware against possible German sabotage. It was feared that the German sabotage apparatus might be far greater than anyone knew, and the Declaration of War might trigger widespread terror. The First Battalion headquarters was at the Wilmington Armory.

Two weeks later, on April 6, the nation was officially at war with the Central powers. Delaware immediately applied to the War Department for authority to organize a third battalion in its regiment so that the entire regiment would be able to go into service as a single unit, rather than as separate battalions, as it had in New Mexico the previous year. Permission was soon obtained, and while the first battalion continued its guard duty, the second immediately went to work recruiting. The recruiters sounded the pitch, "Join up and go with the hometown boys." A favorite ploy was to deny a weekend pass or furlough to any soldier unless he promised to return with a new recruit. The Newark and New Castle companies were assigned the upper part of the state and the Dover and Milford units the lower part.

President Wilson ordered the guard to active federal service on July 15, 1917, in two increments to ameliorate the formidable mustering of 400,000 men all at once. Eleven states were in the initial call-up, and the balance would follow.

The Second Battalion Delaware Guard was held in state service until called by the president on July 25. By August 5, the entire National Guard—379,701 troops—were on active duty at mobilization camps across America. Enough Delaware men had been signed up for a full regiment. The new Third Battalion was officially organized, and the rest of the regiment joined the battalion already on active duty. At this

A National Guard recruiting poster that reads: "Come on Boys, Give the Guard a Fighting Chance!" *Courtesy Library of Congress.*

time, the regiment consisted of three battalions of four companies each: headquarters, supply, machine gun company and sanitary detachment, aggregating 58 officers and 1,349 enlisted men.

Camp McClellan, Alabama

The entire National Guard traveled to warm parts of the country for assembly and training. The movement of around a third of one million men to these camps placed a severe strain on the nation's rail system. In September 1917, the 1st Delaware Regiment received orders to move from the state rifle range below New Castle to Camp McClellan, Alabama. The regiment was assigned to the Twenty-ninth Division, "Blue and Gray," mostly with Maryland; Washington, D.C.; and Virginia Guardsmen. They arrived on October 6 and found a blow to their morale waiting for them. The Delaware regiment was broken up, with most of the men and some of the officers assigned to the 114th Infantry Regiment of the expanded army. Other men were scattered throughout the Twenty-ninth Division, and most of the officers found themselves deprived of their commands and assigned to the Fifty-fourth Depot Brigade.

This was too much for the people of Delaware to take. Even the identity of their unit was being taken away, despite the army's promise that Delaware's regiment would be maintained if the state could furnish three battalions. While the Delaware men froze in tents through one of the coldest winters in Alabama history, deprived even of the minor comfort of freezing with men

Delaware National Guard officers of Company I at Camp Dix, New Jersey. *Courtesy Delaware Public Archives.*

they knew, the people of Delaware went to work. On January 7, 1918, U.S. senator Willard Saulsbury Jr. announced that the army had finally agreed to live up to its original promise, and the men of the First Delaware were to be reassembled in their own unit.

After being forced by politicians to backtrack on their plans, the army found itself unable to deploy the Twenty-ninth Division on schedule, due to the loss of these National Guardsmen. The army retaliated by assigning them the unglamorous task of serving as pioneer infantry, which was formed primarily as an armed labor force for repair and construction. The First Delaware was already in the process of reassembling. By the middle of the month, it had arrived at Camp Dix to begin training as a regiment of a new type, pioneer infantry.

The United States Army formed many pioneer infantry regiments for the Great War. They were cross-trained in combat engineering and infantry tactics. As one of their officers remarked, "They did everything the infantry was too proud to do and the engineers [were] too lazy to do." In those days, the question was frequently asked "what is a pioneer?" Many and varied were the explanations. The military definition of a *pioneer* is: "Pioneers march at the head of each battalion to clear a passage for it through woods or other obstructions, improve roads, make bridges and generally do any minor engineering or construction work that may be necessary."

Camp Dix, New Jersey

No specific information had been given the regiment as to what the duties of pioneer infantry were, so after arriving at Camp Dix, Colonel Reed began training them as regular infantry. On February 27, the First Delaware was officially designated the Fifty-ninth Pioneer Infantry Regiment. The unit strength at that time was 52 officers and 1,663 enlisted men. On March 16, 1918, troops from Company B of the 307th Machine Gun Battalion—a unit of the Seventy-eighth Division, comprising men from Delaware—were transferred to the regiment. On April 1, 293 additional recruits from Delaware arrived at Camp Dix and were assigned to the regiment. More men were assigned to it from the draft in Delaware, and it was finally rounded out to full strength by the addition of recruits from New Jersey and New York. The new men were required because the new type of regiments was considerably larger than the prewar ones. On April 26, 1918, 609 recruits were received, and on July 24, orders were received to fill out the regiment to war strength from the July draft. On August 6, 1918, 1,309 recruits were received from the 153rd Depot Brigade.

The Fifty-ninth Regiment paraded in Philadelphia on April 27, 1918, joining other troops in a demonstration for the Third Liberty Loan bond drive. Colonel Reed was notified on May 7, 1918, that the regiment would proceed overseas.

Three weeks of intensive target practice and field firing ensued for the Fifty-ninth in May and June. Sergeant Anthony Summers of the supply company described the preparations from his perspective:

> Our company had been very busy the last two weeks previous to our departure; working day and night receiving equipment and issuing equipment to the several companies. There was a great scuffling in the various offices as there were service records and all papers containing the pedigree of every man to be carefully checked and rechecked, passenger lists to be made out, and final settlements of company accounts; consolidation of invoices and receipts and final check on property. On August 21, 1918 embarkation orders were received, and on the 23rd of August Governor John G. Townsend Jr., visited the boys at Camp Dix to pay an official farewell to the sons of Delaware. He was joined by the mothers, wives, sweethearts, of the stout-hearted boys before their departure to fight for the virtue of womanhood, and the liberty and independence of the universe.

Summers's account explained, "When the order came on August 27th to pack for overseas, well we had to pack enough to load down an ordinary pack mule, but nevertheless, it was packed. We fell in alongside our barrack in full, heavy, overseas marching order."

The soldiers' kit included: a rifle and its equipment; a haversack and a pack carrier; a cartridge belt; a canteen and cover; an overcoat; a slicker; a shelter half and rope; pins; a pole; a blanket; an extra shirt; a suit of underwear; three pairs of socks; a razor; a shoe brush; a shaving brush; soap; towels; a mirror; a hair brush; a comb; two pairs of shoe strings; an extra pair of hob-nails; a condiment can filled with coffee, sugar and salt; two reserve rations; a mess outfit; and a few personal articles, which included, to a great extent, extra packages of cigarettes. After enjoying a feast and packing two beef sandwiches for the journey, the men of the battalion started to move out in the late evening after a roll call. "[They] swung around 2nd Street and New

Jersey Avenue as eager and proud as any paint besmeared warrior of the ancient forests," according to Summers.

The men from Delaware were now trained, equipped and ready for the fight.

3

A RISING SEA

A MARITIME STATE

Delaware has a coastline the entire length of the state along the Delaware River and Bay estuary and the Atlantic Ocean. In the southwestern corner, rivers connect it to the Chesapeake Bay. It is a state with a maritime

Wilmington shipyards on the Christiana River. This photo was taken just after the war in 1921. *Courtesy Hagley Museum Library.*

heritage that includes fishing, local and international shipping and shipbuilding. It is the gateway to the Philadelphia area and its industrial river valley. Ships have been built along the Delaware River since colonial times. Delaware made a significant contribution to the war effort through its shipbuilding activities.

WILMINGTON SHIPYARDS

Two Wilmington shipyards, Harlan and Hollingsworth and Pusey and Jones, achieved international notoriety when one launched America's first all-iron, ocean-going steamer in 1844, and the other built the nation's first iron sailing ship in 1855. The two Wilmington firms exemplified the emergence of the iron shipbuilding industry.

In the 1860s, Harlan and Hollingsworth and Pusey and Jones led iron shipbuilding firms in the United States. By the 1870s, with the growth of other iron shipbuilding firms on the Delaware, the river became known as the "American Clyde." Both firms developed specialties in small- to medium-sized boats (partly because of the small size of the Christina River), especially ferries, river steamboats and luxury yachts.

By 1883, Harlan and Hollingsworth had a plant covering forty-three acres and a record of over two hundred iron ships built since 1836. Harlan and Hollingsworth had a dry dock capable of taking in a vessel 340 feet in length. Every industry, from miner and workman to architect and engineer, was herein employed—concentrating nearly fifty trades—and had developed from an area of about two acres of ground to a frontage of 2,800 feet on both banks of the Christina River.

The First World War brought Wilmington to prosperity as munitions works, shipbuilders and foundries went into action. Harlan and Hollingsworth built seventy ships during the war and continued to manufacture ships until 1926.

More than two thousand employees worked for Pusey and Jones during the Great War building ships. A second shipyard was added in Gloucester City, New Jersey. But after producing nineteen ships, the name of the yard was changed to the New Jersey Shipbuilding Company.

A third major shipyard, the Jackson and Sharp firm, built grain barges, car floats, lighters, tugs, ferry boats, towboats, schooners and dump scows. While the shipyard kept busy, iron and steel shipbuilding quickly eclipsed wood shipbuilding. Jackson and Sharp produced 15,617 tons of shipping

U.S. subchasers moored in Berehaven Harbour, Bantry Bay, Ireland, in 1918. Numbers 342 to 345 were built by Jackson and Sharp in Wilmington. *Courtesy Shipwrecks of Cork Harbour.*

in 1906, compared to 48,671 tons for Pusey and Jones and 43,016 tons for Harlan and Hollingsworth.

The Jackson and Sharp plant "launched the largest tonnage of wooden boats put out by any American shipyard" between 1914 and 1915. Jackson and Sharp was contracted in 1917 to build eight wooden submarine chasers. About one hundred men did the job within six months. Boat repair at the shipyard took on added importance during the war. Jackson and Sharp also produced a variety of rail cars, acid buckets and powder trays for the DuPont Powder Company's munitions work. The plant also manufactured tables, benches and pontoons.

DOWNSTATE SHIPYARDS

Small shipyards downstate also enjoyed the bounty of government contracts during the war. They built predominately small wooden ships. William G. Abbott of Milford, the state's primary builder of wooden schooners during this period, registered twelve vessels at the Port of Wilmington between 1900 and 1920. These vessels ranged in size from a sloop of fourteen tons to a four-masted schooner of over seven hundred tons. John Moore and the Smith and Terry Company, both of Bethel along the Nanticoke River, continued to build ships into the second quarter of the century. A few manufacturers, such as the Vinyard Shipbuilding Company of Milford, maintained a steady business with the construction of pleasure craft, some of which were repurposed as patrol craft. The Vinyard Shipbuilding Company in Milford, Delaware, built submarine chasers SC-144, 145 and 146. The SC-144 was one of the first to join the patrol group at Cape May. The SC-145 operated with the patrol group out of Lewes, and the SC-146 was sent to France.

DELAWARE RIVER SHIPBUILDING BASEBALL LEAGUE

The war wasn't all toil and effort. Recreation played an important role in maintaining morale. This was as important in the civilian community as it was among those in uniform. Among the most popular were the shipyard baseball leagues.

Baseball leagues flourished in American shipyards during World War I as legions of workers built warships and troop transports to safeguard the Atlantic sea lanes and carry men and materiel to Europe. According to Jim Leeke in an article published in the 2013 *National Pastime*, among the best of these circuits was the Delaware River Shipbuilding League of 1918. Centered in Philadelphia, it represented eight shipyards operating along the river in Delaware, New Jersey and Pennsylvania, including the Wilmington firms Harlan and Hollingsworth and Pusey and Jones.

The Harlan and Hollingsworth baseball team, pennant winner of the Delaware River Shipyards League. Centerfielder "Shoeless" Joe Jackson is ninth from the left, standing. *Courtesy Shoeless Joe Jackson Museum, Greenville, SC.*

The Delaware River League had about two dozen recent or retired big leaguers on its rosters, most of them journeyman players. Any big-league player who sought a shipyard job in 1918 heard abuse from many fans and sportswriters. A former St. Louis player serving in the navy saw the phenomenon firsthand in a shipyard game featuring several ex-Giants. "Nothing was too mean to call them," he wrote, "and if they got a dollar for every time some one called them 'slackers' or 'trench-dodgers' they must have gotten round-shouldered carrying their money home."

On May 13, a Selective Service board in South Carolina notified Joe Jackson, of the champion Chicago White Sox, that it had reclassified his draft status. "Shoeless Joe" was suddenly set to join the next group to be called for military service.

The next morning, however, at the urging of his wife, Jackson instead reported for work as a painter at the Harlan yard in Wilmington, a subsidiary of mighty Bethlehem Steel. Shipyard workers, like those in other vital war industries, were usually exempt from military service. Although the outfielder was illiterate, the shipyard not only accepted Jackson, it also immediately promoted him to painting inspector.

"The stories that all ball player workmen at $500 a month have to do is punch a clock in the morning is false," *Sporting News* reported. "With very few exceptions' everyone [*sic*] of them does a full day's work. Furthermore, he praises the efforts that have been made to make baseball the main recreation for the ship yard [*sic*] workers."

The league continued to increasing crowds and growing success. The Chester, Pennsylvania team had the pennant nearly sewn up in late July. However, there was a team eligibility controversy regarding some of its players. After a ruling by the league secretary, the season ended with Chester, Harlan and Hog Island in a three-way tie. The tie wasn't broken on the diamond but rather in corporate meeting rooms. An eligibility committee issued a ruling on August 22, taking victories away from both Chester and Hog Island. As a result, the Chester club plummeted from atop the standings with a record of 12-2 to fourth place at 8-6. Harlan was suddenly tied with New York Ship, both with revised 11-3 records.

Harlan easily won the playoff game, 5–0. Jackson played centerfield, went one for three at the plate, walked once and scored a run. One *Chester Times* headline read: "With Joe Jackson the Wilmington Bunch Grabs Play-off." The playoff victory sent Harlan into a best-of-five series for the championship of Atlantic Coast shipyards.

"The Harlans looked like a beaten team until Jackson, who is suffering with an injured right foot, took Dumont's place at bat in the ninth," the *New*

York Sun reported. Shoeless Joe "slammed out a hard drive down the first base line for a single," the *Inquirer* added. "Jackson could have easily made a two-bagger out of the hit if it had not been for his injured foot, as it was all he could do to reach first." The single started a rally that brought Harlan a 3–2 victory.

The series shifted north to the Polo Grounds the following day. In a steady drizzle, and with Jackson out of the lineup, the old Chicago battery of Williams and Lynn held Standard scoreless before four thousand fans. The Wilmington team went for the sweep back in Philadelphia on September 14. Jackson returned to the Harlan lineup before 4,500 fans, doubled and homered twice off former Cardinals and Dodgers pitcher Dan Griner. "Shoeless Joe was a whole show in himself," the *Public Ledger* marveled.

The 4–0, two-hit victory by Williams gave Harlan and Hollingsworth the Atlantic Coast Shipyard championship. This final, stirring game was also the brightest moment in the league's brief history.

When the First World War ended with the armistice, many shipyards downsized or closed by the following spring. The Delaware River

The Wilson Line ferry *Brandywine. Courtesy Delaware Historical Society.*

Shipbuilding League briefly fielded six amateur teams before folding in 1919. Shoeless Joe Jackson returned to Charles Comiskey's big-league club in Chicago, where their names were to be forever tarred by the Black Sox scandal.

FERRY LINES

World War I triggered significant industrial expansion on the Lower Delaware. The DuPont powder works received enormous war orders and had to open new facilities at several sites in New Jersey to meet increased product demand. Thousands of powder workers from the tri-state region were recruited for the new plants located in the vicinity of Penn's Grove, New Jersey. The majority of the Pennsylvania and Delaware workers took Wilson Line ferries across the Delaware River to Penn's Grove to get to work. By 1916, the Penn's Grove ferries alone were making sixteen sailings daily. Two separate ferry entities, Christina Ferry Company and the Wilmington and Penn's Grove Transportation Company were established to accommodate this new traffic. New ferry piers had to be built at Deepwater Point and Carneys Point, New Jersey. Overwhelmed by this new traffic, the Wilson Line purchased several steamers to handle the new ferry service load. During peak years, steamboats and ferries made more than thirty Wilson Line sailings from Wilmington every day.

NAVAL SECTION BASE AT CAPE HENLOPEN

Few realize the scope of the large naval facility that made its home in Delaware during the Great War. In 1914, the war in Europe was raging, and it was possible that the United States would be drawn into the war. Precautions were being taken to defend shipping in the approaches to Delaware Bay. Naval Section Bases were established on Cape Henlopen and Cape May. Almost all traces of the Henlopen naval facility have long since disappeared.

William H.J. Manthorpe Jr., in his comprehensive history of the U.S. Navy at Cape Henlopen, describes the naval response to the threat of war at the Delaware Capes in his book, *A Century of Service: The U.S. Navy on Cape Henlopen, Lewes, Delaware: 1898–1996*:

A "Naval Section Base" is a shore base under the overall command of a Naval District Commandant, as distinguished from a "Naval Base" or "Naval Operating Base" which are under the command of a Fleet Commander.

At Cape Henlopen, the planned closing of the existing Public Health Service Delaware Breakwater Quarantine Hospital was deferred and the hospital continued at a reduced level of operations. The suitability of that facility and its piers as a naval base had been demonstrated in August 1914 when two destroyers on neutrality patrol stopped there and, again, when, over the Christmas–New Year's period of 1914–1915, the battleship USS Ohio was quarantined there.

As the U.S. entered the war, in April 1917, the Cape was defined by Presidential Executive Order as a "defensive sea area." A Navy delegation met with the mayor of Lewes to make arrangements for the Navy to occupy the former quarantine hospital facilities and piers as a Naval Section Base, under the command of the Commandant of the Fourth Naval District.

By the Spring of 1918, the headquarters and administrative offices had been moved to the Lewes Coast Guard Station. The principal part of the base occupied the piers, and administrative buildings of the former quarantine hospital while the hospital barracks became the base enlisted living quarters (BEQ).

There were about 800 men stationed at the base. The accommodations at the base were quite primitive. Nevertheless, life was not all hard for the sailors assigned. The Bay provided recreation close at hand, the band provided lively entertainment and there was a YMCA on base. The sailors who did get into Lewes were treated well. The Rector of St. Peter's Church made his Rectory a home for the men and had a dozen to fifty lodgers a night.

Naval Section Base Lewes was established primarily to serve as home to the varied organizations and personnel responsible for the routing, control and support of the vast numbers of naval combatants and transports that would soon be en-route from Philadelphia to Europe.

Among the first convoys to form up at the Cape in June 1917 was one of cruisers and transports, including the Navy transport USS Hancock (AP-4), carrying the Fifth Marine Brigade to join the American Expeditionary Force in France.

The first naval force based at the Section Base Lewes was the minesweeping section. The section was composed of steam-powered, wooden-hulled vessels from the menhaden fishing fleets that operated in waters adjacent to the

Delaware Breakwater. The largest of these was the *Delaware*, acquired from the Delaware Fish Oil Company of Lewes. The *Delaware* was taken by the navy in May 1917, converted as a minesweeper and placed in commission as the USS *Delaware* (SP-467). At least nine other Delaware Bay menhaden fishing vessels were purchased outright, rapidly converted for minesweeping service at the Philadelphia Navy Yard, commissioned into the navy and assigned to Lewes.

While the minesweeping section was being formed at Lewes, the patrol section was being formed at Cape May. The patrol section consisted mainly of private yachts acquired by donation or purchase from individual owners. They were converted for navy use, equipped with weapons—generally a main battery of a single pedestal-mounted gun and a secondary battery of a machine gun as well as depth charges—and commissioned.

Most patrol craft were based at Cape May, but at least two were based at Lewes: the USS *Drusilla* (SP-372), which had been acquired from the Philadelphia millionaire Anthony J. Drexel, and the USS *Juniata* (SP-603). Patrol craft monitored the shipping lanes approaching the cape and at the harbor entrance. The Lewes units served as guard ships in the harbor and on neutrality duty.

With the signing of the armistice, all war activities ceased. Convoys and patrols were suspended, and district vessels were decommission and returned to their respective owners. The base at Lewes was abandoned, and demobilization was begun and carried out promptly. The military and civilian personnel were demobilized (transferred or discharged).

War Comes to Delaware Shores

Submarines were sighted in local waters on May 20, 1918. At the end of May, the U-151 *Deutschland* laid a cluster of mines off Cape Henlopen and continued north to cut a transatlantic cable off New York. Then, on June 2, what came to be called "Black Sunday," the sub sank three more schooners and three steamships and damaged two other ships off the coast of New Jersey, about fifty miles southeast of Barnegat Light.

The largest was the *Carolina*, which was torpedoed off New Jersey, killing thirteen out of the three hundred passengers and crew. The British steamer *Appleby* brought nineteen numb survivors into Lewes where the local residents were shocked by their woeful conditions.

The following day, the tanker *Herbert L. Pratt* broadcast that it had been torpedoed three miles off Cape Henlopen, literally within sight of shore. It had been en route to Philadelphia. The Lewes pilot boat *Philadelphia* soon arrived to evacuate crewmen. Some remained aboard and, with a salvage crew, righted the ship. Two warships and a flotilla of smaller boats rushed to its assistance. On closer inspection, it was found to have struck a mine in its forward section. It was towed to the Delaware breakwater by this armada of rescuers.

In the resulting confusion, a lookout reported the wake of a submarine, and a wild goose chase ensued. Every vessel that had a weapon blasted away at the phantom submarine, and the roar of gunfire rattled window panes on Second Street in Lewes. Not since the War of 1812 had war been this close and menacing to the townspeople.

At the breakwater, the *Pratt* was quickly refloated by attaching pontoons, towed by the salvage tug USS *Tasco* to the pier at the section base where the ship was righted, the hole patched and power restored. *Pratt* was able to sail to Philadelphia under its own power. William H.J. Manthorpe Jr. said:

> In the belief that a submarine was in the area, search operations were begun. Soon section base minesweepers located and destroyed three mines. With the mine threat identified, the Commanding Officer of the Section Base was directed to stop all outgoing vessels and the port of Philadelphia was closed temporarily until such time as the Commandant was assured that the channels to sea were safe and free from mines. Several Fleet minesweepers—USS Widgeon (AM-22), USS Teal (AM-23) and USS Kingfisher (AM-25)—moved from Philadelphia to Lewes.
>
> In July and August, three other Deutschland-type subs operated in the Cape area. U-156 sunk one ship off northern New Jersey before moving north. U-140 sunk one ship further at sea before moving south.
>
> Next U-117, nearing the middle of what had already been a very successful cruise, entered Cape area waters, sinking one tanker and then another off Barnegat Light and then laying mines in the area.
>
> On the way south past the Cape the sub was attacked by a Navy plane and subchaser. After escaping to sink a small coastal schooner, U-117 laid more mines in the area of Fenwick Light. She then moved south to create more havoc.
>
> On 18 September, a month after U-117 had left the area, the USS Minnesota (BB-22), an older battleship serving as a training ship, hit

one of the mines laid by U-117 off of the Fenwick lightship. The ship was able to contain the damage and proceed to the Cape and Philadelphia under her own power.

But, even long after U-117 had departed, the effects of her visit remained. Two merchant ships were sunk in October off Barnegat Inlet by the mines that U-117 had laid earlier. Then, just as the war was ending, on 9 November, USS Saetia *(ID No. 2317) a Navy support cargo ship encountered another of U-117's mines and sunk 10 miles southeast of Fenwick Island Shoal. All eighty-five hands survived to come ashore at Ocean City and Cape May.*

Some of the mines laid by U-151 and U-117 were still being found in early 1919.

Submarines and mines were not the only hazards to shipping during the war. The naval tug *Cherokee* was caught at sea in a gale on February 27, 1918. Its crew of forty men gallantly fought a fifty-mile-per hour wind in the aging hulk, which had never been designed for blue water cruising. It was headed south from Philadelphia. Off Fenwick Island, its steering gear broke, and it floundered in the seas. The wireless operator kept in touch until the seas closed over him. Ten men scrambled onto one life raft and four onto another. Two were washed off the second raft, and two more later died. All ten survivors were semiconscious when the British tanker *Admiral* rescued them. Thirty crewmen were lost.

The *City of Athens* was a passenger liner going from New York to Savannah along the Delaware coast early on the foggy morning of May 1, 1918. It carried sixty-eight passengers and sixty-six crew members, mostly asleep in their cabins. The French destroyer *La Glorie* loomed out of the mist on a collision course, its bow smashing into the bow of the *City of Athens.* Everyone in the fore part of the *Athens* was killed, and fire erupted, only to be smothered by the incoming rush of water. An SOS was sent from the radio shack, but the *Athens* sank within four minutes. *La Glorie* launched lifeboats to pick up survivors still dressed in nightclothes. The passenger list included twenty-four U.S. Marines, of whom seven perished. The total death toll was tallied at sixty-nine, with sixty-five surviving.

USS DELAWARE

The name of Delaware was carried to the seas by a navy battleship. The USS *Delaware* (BB-28) was launched on February 6, 1909, by Newport News Shipbuilding Company and commissioned on April 4, 1910, with Captain C.A. Gove in command. It was the first of America's dreadnought class of battleships, and when it was launched, the *Delaware* was the most powerful vessel in the world.

After visiting Wilmington, Delaware, from October 3 to October 9, 1910, to receive a gift of a silver service from the state. The *Delaware* sailed from Hampton Roads on November 1 with the First Division, Atlantic Fleet, to assume its peacetime duties. It visited Weymouth, England, and Cherbourg, France, and after battle practice at Guantanamo Bay, Cuba, returned to Norfolk on January 18, 1911.

With the outbreak of World War I in Europe, the *Delaware* returned to Hampton Roads from winter maneuvers in the Caribbean to train armed guard crews and engineers, as well as to join in exercises to ready the fleet for war. On November 25, 1917, it sailed with the Ninth Division, bound for Scapa Flow, Scotland. After battling bad weather in the North Atlantic, it joined the Sixth Battle Squadron, British Grand Fleet, on December 14 for exercises to coordinate the operations of the Allied forces.

The Sixth Battle Squadron got underway on February 6, 1918, with an escort of eight British destroyers to convoy a large group of merchant ships to Norway. Cruising off Stavanger two days later, the *Delaware* was reported to have been attacked twice by a submarine, but each time, skillful handling enabled the battleship to evade the torpedoes. The squadron returned to its home base at Scapa Flow on February 10. Delaware participated in two more convoy voyages in March and April and then sailed with the Grand Fleet on April 24 to reinforce the Second Battle Cruiser Squadron, which was on convoy duty and expected contact with the enemy. Only the vessels of the advance screen made any contact, and the chance for action faded.

From June 30 to July 2, 1918, the Sixth Battle Squadron, with a division of British destroyers as escort, went to sea to screen American ships laying the North Sea mine barrage. On July 22, King George V of England inspected the ships of the Grand Fleet at Rosyth, Scotland, and eight days later, after being relieved by the *Arkansas* (BB-33), the *Delaware* sailed for Hampton Roads, arriving on August 12.

The *Delaware* remained at York River until November 12, 1918, and then sailed to Boston Navy Yard for an overhaul. After routine sea duty hosting midshipmen sea cruises and exercising with the fleet, the *Delaware* entered

Battleship USS *Delaware* (BB-28) anchored at Guantanamo Bay, Cuba. *Courtesy U.S. Naval Historical Center.*

Norfolk Navy Yard on August 30, 1923. Its crew was transferred to the USS *Colorado* (BB-45), a newly commissioned battleship assigned to replace the *Delaware* in the fleet. Moving to Boston Navy Yard in September, it was stripped of warlike equipment and decommissioned on November 10, 1923. The *Delaware* was sold on February 5, 1924, and scrapped in accordance with the Washington Treaty on the limitation of armaments.

4

SHELTER FROM
THE STORM

P art of the preparation for war was to deploy defensive measures. Defending the homeland was paramount, and the United States felt itself threatened by a belligerent who employed saboteurs, U-boats and other underhanded methods. There remained the possibility of a foreign incursion.

STATE DEFENSE FORCES

In peacetime, the National Guard commander is the state governor, and the National Guard is a resource for civil emergency, natural disaster relief and other state needs. Yet in wartime, the National Guard can be federalized and become a national asset commanded by the president to defend the country. During World War I, the question arose: if the National Guard is federalized and deployed, then who would see to the traditional mission needs of the state?

During the preparedness period just prior to United States involvement in World War I, Congress consented to establishing home defense forces for the states in the event that the National Guard was federalized. Consequently, Delaware formed a home defense force to fill the void left by its deployed guardsmen. According to the December 31, 1918 *Biennial Report of the Adjutant General, Delaware* by I.P. Wickersham:

In accordance with General Order No. 10 this office, as amended by General Order No. 21, December 21, 1917, providing for the organization of Companies of Infantry for duty within the state, I have to report that one Company together with a Supply Detachment, aggregating four officers and seventy-one enlisted men has been organized and stationed in Wilmington. This Company is well uniformed, armed, equipped and instructed. The officers and men of this company are to be commended for their attention to their military duties, having responded for drill two evenings each week for the past year.

Additionally, the national U.S. Guard, which came to number 26,000, was culled from the ranks of those deemed unfit for overseas deployment. Its purpose was to oversee internal security and was established by the War Department as a facsimile of Britain's Home Guard. By 1918, over 100,000 men were serving in forty-two state guards. Rather than use the militia to build the regular army, during the war, the military relied primarily on draft calls to fill the huge manpower requirement required of the army, formally established in July 1918.

FORTIFICATIONS AND COASTAL BATTERIES

As a coastal state with an extended shoreline along the Delaware River and Bay, Delaware has had a long history of various incursions, piracy and the threat of invasion from foreign powers. The Delaware estuary leads to the wealthy and important cities of New Castle and Wilmington, Delaware; Philadelphia and Chester, Pennsylvania; and Camden and Trenton, New Jersey. From the very start, European settlers erected fortifications to guard this highway to the sea. These original strongholds were places where the local populace could shelter from Native Americans or rival powers.

These tiny colonial outposts eventually were superseded by stronger fortifications meant to defend the maritime approaches to the colonies from French and Spanish privateers and, during the War of Independence, against the British. The fortifications were not always successful.

By the Civil War, the coastal defense of the Delaware River relied on forts at the mouth of the Delaware River. Fort Delaware, located on Pea Patch Island was the keystone, flanked by Fort DuPont at the mouth of the Chesapeake and Delaware Canal in Delaware City and Fort Mott in New Jersey (built postwar). These three forts had overlapping fields of fire and prevented the approach of the enemy beyond their gates. They were steadily improved as newer technology provided longer-range guns. This remained the situation on the eve of World War I.

FORT DELAWARE was originally constructed in 1817 as a replacement for Fort Mifflin, which was deemed too close to Philadelphia to provide an effective defense in delaying invaders. A fortification farther down river would also provide protection for other vital port cities such as Chester, Marcus Hook, Wilmington and New Castle. On February 7, 1821, the board of engineers reported:

> *In the Delaware, the fort on the Pea Patch Island, and one on the Delaware shore opposite, defend the water passage as far below Philadelphia as localities will permit: They force an enemy to land forty miles below the city to attack it by land, and thus afford time for the arrival of succors…The two projected forts will also have the advantages of covering the canal destined to connect the Chesapeake with the Delaware.*

The boggy soil of this midriver island presented huge construction challenges, requiring the driving of over 7,400 piles over a period of two years (1849 to 1851). The muddy soil yielded to sand at the depth of forty feet. A star-shaped fort was superseded by a polygonal and then a pentagonal design of stone, brick and concrete. A fire destroyed an early design in 1831, and subsequently, the fort suffered from a hurricane in 1878. A tornado in 1885 did major damage to the frame structures dotted around the island.

Fort Delaware served its purpose as a deterrent and never fired a shot in anger. It became more infamous as a prison facility for Confederate soldiers during the Civil War. By August 1863, there were more than 11,000 prisoners on the island; by war's end, it had held almost 33,000 men. The conditions were decent by nineteenth-century standards; however, about 2,500 prisoners died at Fort Delaware.

During the late 1890s, new gun batteries were constructed at Fort Delaware. These batteries were part of a program initiated by the Endicott Board, a group headed by the secretary of war, William C. Endicott. Instead of many guns concentrated in a traditional thick-walled masonry structure, the Endicott batteries are spread out over a wide area, concealed behind concrete parapets flush with the surrounding terrain.

In 1896, half of the soldier barracks and a set of officer quarters were demolished inside the fort. The parade ground was excavated and thousands

An aerial view looking south of Fort Delaware on Pea Patch Island in the Delaware River near Delaware City. *Courtesy Library of Congress.*

of piles were steam driven to support a foundation for a concrete three-gun battery as a way to modernize the defenses protecting ports along the Delaware River.

Following a period of caretaking status, the fort was garrisoned for a brief time during the Great War. Nearby Fort DuPont was the main defense site, with Fort Delaware and Fort Mott serving as a sub-posts, according to army records. In March 1919, soldiers began the process of mothballing the old fort, removing everything except items pertaining to the three twelve-inch guns of Battery Torbert, according to Private James C. Davis, a Fort DuPont soldier who worked on the detail. By the end of the Great War, Fort Saulsbury in Milford, Delware, was near completion, and its longer-range guns rendered the three upriver forts secondary lines of defense.

FORT DUPONT is located between Delaware City and the Chesapeake and Delaware Canal. The first fortification built was the Ten Gun Battery, an auxiliary to nearby Fort Delaware during the American Civil War. A twenty-gun battery was constructed on the reservation during the 1870s followed by a mine control casemate in 1892.

During the Spanish-American War and the following few years, major construction took place to upgrade the defense capabilities of the three forts defending the major ports along the Delaware River. Construction took place at Forts Mott, Delaware and DuPont in the form of Endicott-era batteries that mounted long-range rifles, mortars and rapid fire guns. On July 22, 1899, Army General Orders, No. 134, officially designated "the battery at Delaware City" as Fort DuPont, named in honor of Rear Admiral Samuel Francis Du Pont.

During World War I, Fort DuPont continued serving the role of coastal defense as well as training post for local draftees and deploying artillery units. Following the war, the long-range guns in Batteries Read and Gibson were dismounted and shipped elsewhere. Units such as the Seventh Trench Mortar Battalion used the site for basic and advanced training before heading to France in October 1918.

In 1922, the post became headquarters for the First Engineer Regiment, which garrisoned the post until 1941. During World War II, Fort DuPont served as a mobilization station for deploying units and contained a prisoner-of-war camp for captured German soldiers and sailors. After the war, Fort DuPont was declared surplus.

FORT MOTT in New Jersey was part of a three-fort defense system designed for the Delaware River during the modernization period following the American Civil War. The other two forts in the system were Fort Delaware on Pea Patch Island and Fort DuPont in Delaware City.

Original plans for Fort Mott specified eleven gun emplacements with twenty guns and a mortar battery with six emplacements for six more Rodman smoothbore guns. Construction was started in 1872; however, only two of the gun emplacements and two magazines in the mortar battery were completed by 1876, when all work stopped.

War Department Order, No. 72, issued on December 16, 1897, designated the new fort as Fort Mott in honor of Major General Gershom Mott of Trenton, New Jersey, a distinguished veteran of the Mexican American and Civil Wars.

Fort Mott became obsolete as the principal defensive installation on the Delaware River with the construction of Fort Saulsbury—near Milford, Delaware—shortly after the Great War. The steadily increasing range and accuracy of the Coast Artillery resulted in moving the defense of the Delaware River progressively further down the bay.

FORT SAULSBURY is located about six miles outside Milford, Delaware, in the town of Slaughter Beach. The U.S. Army approached David W. Shockley and Mark H. Shockley about purchasing their land (about 161 acres) for use as a fort in 1917. After more than a year of study by various agencies within the War Department, the construction of the two batteries began in late 1917. The army decided that this particular location was the best available to ensure protection of the mouth of the Delaware Bay and River from any possible enemy threats during World War I.

The fort's mission was to defend the Greater Delaware Valley against potential attacks from the sea. Its four great twelve-inch Howitzer guns had a range of fifteen to twenty miles and were designed to cover the bay entrance and the anchorage from enemy surface and underwater vessels. World War I intelligence indicated that German forces were planning an attack up the Delaware Bay to destroy the industrial areas of Wilmington and Philadelphia. The two batteries of Fort Saulsbury, each with two twelve-inch gun emplacements, would provide defense against such an attack. Impressive as this may sound, the guns were still not a match for the latest battleships at sea, which were able to mount as many as twelve fourteen- or sixteen-inch guns.

In 1918, the fort was completed very near the end of the Great War. The fort included four twelve-inch guns capable of firing two-thousand-pound shells twenty miles and two dirt and grass-covered concrete casements. The casements were constructed of fourteen-foot-thick steel reinforced concrete with six feet of earth on top for camouflage. The fort was named for Delaware senator Willard Saulsbury Sr., who served in the U.S. Senate from 1859 through 1871.

The huge battery bunkers were constructed of steel and reinforced concrete. On top of each bunker, there was a concrete trench connecting an observation post located at each end of the mound. A spiral staircase at each end was used to reach the observation posts from inside the mound.

Since the fort was completed so close to the end of the Great War, it was never fully manned. The garrison numbered about thirty soldiers and officers during the initial operational period. After the armistice in November 1918, the fort was manned by only six to eight soldiers with the ranking soldier being a sergeant.

An even tinier sub-post was established at Cape Henlopen as the Coast Artillery Detachment Barracks in 1918.

Fort Saulsbury briefly served as a German and Italian prisoner-of-war camp during World War II. Two of its big guns were moved to Fort Miles at Cape Henlopen during World War II. Fort Saulsbury was inactivated and sold to a private party after World War II. It had been among the very last coastal fortifications to be constructed in the United States, and remains a singular unaltered example of its type.

The various fortresses along the Delaware River and Bay proved to be more useful as staging areas, training grounds and housing for troops during the Great War rather than for coastal defense. No serious threat ever materialized from the enemy.

5

THE TEMPEST

OVER THERE

Over 10,000 Delawareans served in uniform during World War I, and many more were volunteers in the Red Cross and in war industries at home. Two significant groups stand out by numbers alone. The Delaware National Guard's Fifty-ninth Pioneer Infantry Regiment deployed about 3,500 hometown citizen-soldiers to France (about half from Delaware). Another overlooked group were the 1,400 African Americans who served as individuals in various segregated units throughout the army.

An African American soldier readies to deploy, posed before Old Glory. *Courtesy Library of Congress.*

African American Contribution

African Americans quickly supported President Wilson's call for support of the war effort. W.E.B. DuBois wrote in the July 1918 issue of the NAACP magazine *Crisis*:

> *We of the colored race have no ordinary interest in the outcome, that which the German power represents today shall spell death to the aspirations of Negroes and all darker races for equality, freedom and democracy. Let us...close ranks shoulder to shoulder with our own white fellow citizens and allied nations that are fighting for democracy.*

Some 400,000 African Americans served in World War I, about half of them deployed overseas. Joseph P. Hickey, in his treatise "Race and War in Delaware," records that about 1,400 of Delaware's soldiers were African American, and 37 African Americans are listed among Delaware's war dead, the majority from the influenza outbreak. These black soldiers served as stevedores, gravediggers and kitchen workers—all menial tasks for those deemed "not good enough, loyal enough, or smart enough to participate in combat." African American soldiers were widely treated with distain, derision and discrimination. They suffered at home under Jim Crow laws and in uniform under a white leadership that offered them little opportunity.

However, in France, they encountered other blacks from the French colonies who were treated with respect by the French soldiers and French citizens. Their treatment overseas brought a realization that things could be different from their experience back home. Their mistreatment in the army became a self-fulfilling prophecy as they were criticized for their weak contribution to the war. Nevertheless, they earned medals and the respect of some. They persevered and were better prepared to suffer the discrimination they would face back home. Hickey wrote:

> *They had met and bonded with other black soldiers from across the country and were strengthened in their pursuit of equality. Most, especially those in Kent and Sussex Counties didn't "voice much opinion" and resumed their pre-military lives, but now they had an inner source of strength that would emerge in the next generation.*

W.E.B. DuBois wrote another editorial in *Crisis* entitled "Returning Soldier":

> *By the God of Heaven, we are cowards and jackasses if now that the war is over, we do not marshal every ounce of our brain and brawn to fight the forces of hell in our own land. We return. We return from fighting. We return fighting! Make way for democracy! We saved it in France and by the great Jehovah, we will save it in the United States of America, or know the reason why.*

Thousands of Delawareans served in the army, navy, Coast Guard and marines as volunteers and as draftees. Among these, the largest single contingent to go to war was the Delaware National Guard.

THE FIFTY-NINTH PIONEER INFANTRY REGIMENT DEPLOYS FOR FRANCE

The Delaware National Guard had been mobilized only six weeks after returning from duty on the Mexican border in early 1917. These men spent over a year guarding the homefront and then training in Alabama and New Jersey before shipping out to France in the summer of 1918.

The troopship *Leviathan* putting to sea with thousands of troops from Hoboken, New Jersey. *Courtesy Library of Congress.*

The Voyage

The Fifty-ninth Pioneer Infantry Regiment traveled by rail from Fort Dix to Hoboken, New Jersey, on the night of August 27, 1918. Several large camouflaged ships at anchor greeted them. These were dwarfed by the largest ship in the world at that time, the *Leviathan*, formerly the German liner *Vaterland*. The men landed at the Hoboken pier around 6:00 a.m. just as it began to rain. They were ushered into a closed passageway, where the Red Cross served them hot coffee and rolls. The Pioneers were also given two postcards, inscribed, "The boat on which I sailed has arrived safely overseas." These cards were to be filled out as the men boarded the ship, so they could be mailed on arrival. The soldiers queued up for embarkation at around 9:00 a.m. on the gangplank of the *Leviathan*, where an officer called each man by name and issued a billeting assignment ticket for the passage. The ship was 954 feet long and had a 100-foot beam with fourteen decks. Each compartment held up to 225 men in canvas bunks, three deep. The weather was very hot with minimal air circulation below decks. The soldiers lined up for mess and marched into the vast dining room, which had formerly been a dance hall and entertainment saloon. They "thought they would melt," according to Sergeant Summer's diary. The men attempted to bathe to cool off, but complained that the salt water would not lather their soap and relief seemed impossible.

On Saturday, August 30, at about 2:00 p.m., the soldiers were ordered on deck with their life preservers. The ships whistle shrieked, and everyone was relieved that they were about to get underway. Some twenty tugs were needed to maneuver the giant ship down the roads from its mooring. The men enjoyed the New York Harbor scenery and the fresh breeze. They especially enjoyed the sight of the Statue of Liberty as they bid their goodbyes to home and country. The topic of conversation was described as, "How long again will it be before we will again see you, Miss Liberty?" The Pioneers were cheered by the sight of ferryboats whose passengers would doff their hats and cheer at the sight of the soldiers going off to war. They sailed out of the harbor to meet their escort of torpedo boat destroyers, submarine chasers and submarines, with airplanes and balloons overhead. The *Leviathan*'s passage through the seas began to move the circulating air throughout the ship, to the relief of the men.

With the ship underway, the men were ordered back to their compartments, where they washed for their meal. The food was described as first class and plentiful, but the men were fed only twice a day due to the

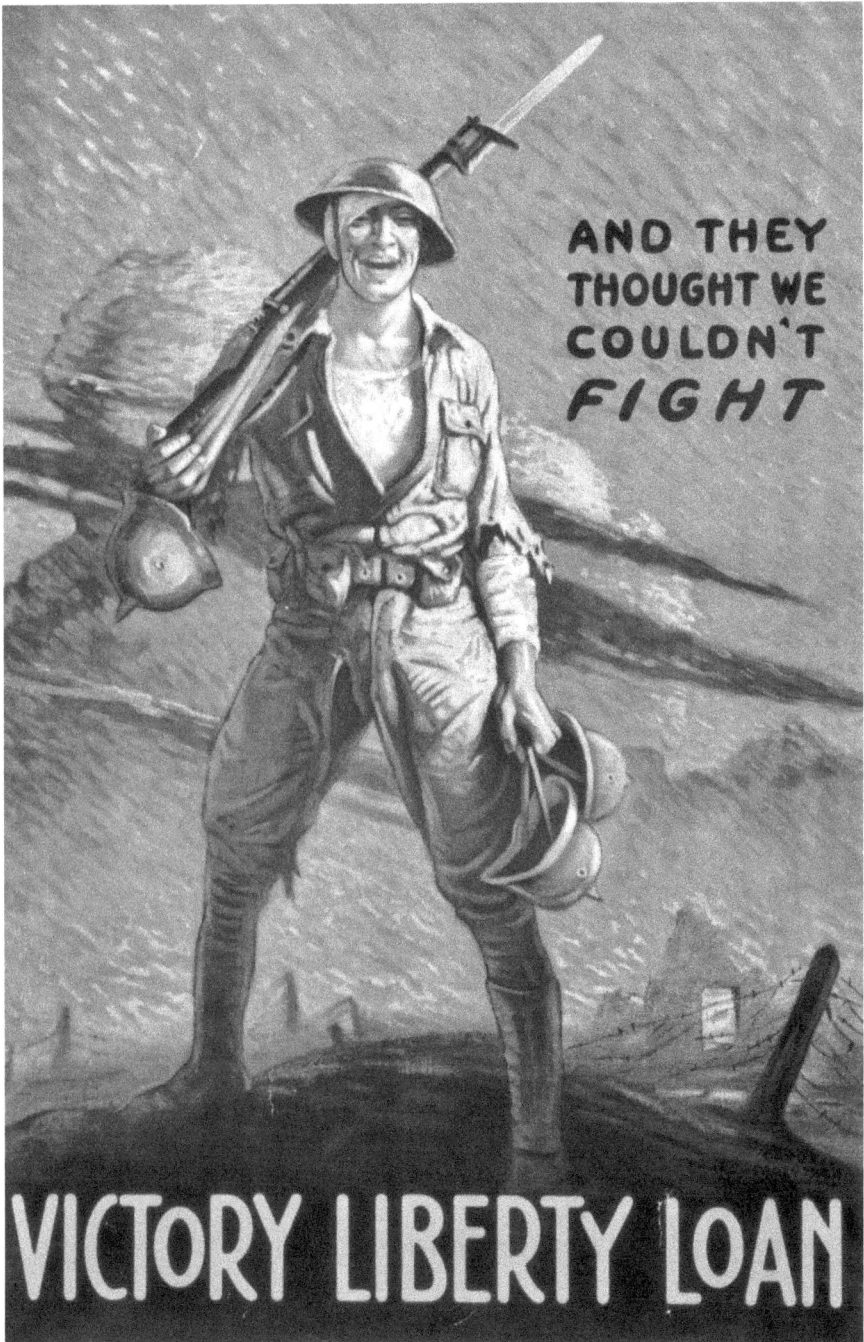

A Liberty loan poster depicting a doughboy at the front. *Courtesy Library of Congress.*

crowded conditions on board. Most of the men turned in early because few had enjoyed any sleep the night before because of the heat and humidity in port. Nevertheless, some were relatively sleepless because they dreamt of submarines, torpedoes and other menaces. But most were comforted by the plentiful six-inch guns mounted all over the boat. Some of the boys were seasick, homesick or "scare sick" from their briny voyage. Sergeant Summer's diary describes them:

> *Those who would entertain themselves by viewing portraits of mother, sister or sweetie. The scare-sick would moan and groan all day and cry at night, when a crowd would gather to discuss the probability of a submarine attack, or whenever one of the six-inchers would belch forth and clear the rust from its barrel. He would keel over and ask for medical aid, or request a chaplain for a last conversation with the sky-pilot.*

The monotony of the voyage was broken somewhat by a daily abandon ship drill. At the sound of a bugle, the men would assemble on the deck with their life preservers and a canteen of water each, usually within ten minutes of the alarm. The soldiers would remain on deck for an hour or two and gaze at the ocean and clouds with an occasional sighting of a school of fish or a fleet of ships.

The voyage took seven days, and the *Leviathan* sailed past the mountainous cliffs of the French coast around 5:00 p.m. on Saturday, September 7, at the Brest Harbor, where it dropped anchor for the night. All the seasick, homesick and scared sick soldiers were at once made whole, laughing and chatting heartily. The next day after breakfast, the men disembarked on a barge to take them ashore in France for the first time. The *Leviathan* was too large to moor at the pier. The men bore witness to a huge ship in the distance, the *Mount Vernon* (formerly the German liner *Kronprinzessin Cecilie*), which had been torpedoed a few days previous with the loss of some thirty-six lives. Owing to the watertight compartments, the *Mount Vernon* was able to return to port.

The Fifty-ninth in France

The Pioneers landed and lined up at the railroad, where a series of boxcars mounted on high wheels labeled "Hommes 40, Chevaux 8," which translated means "40 men, 8 horses"—a phrase that every soldier who has ever been to France will never forget. The men marched through the port of Brest as children came out to ask for pennies. The children also sang a pretty fair rendition of "Hail, Hail, the Gang's All Here" in good English. A description from the First Pioneer Regiment's official history describes Brest in July 1918:

At last we came in view of the rocky Breton coast, a great war balloon floating high above the cliffs and red-sailed fisher boats skimming over the waves. We dropped anchor in Brest harbor and we could see the old gray city lying among the hills, and the ancient castle frowning over the harbor. We were at last in France. It seemed hard to believe that our great adventure had progressed so far. On landing the regiment was marched through Brest, its hilly streets bordered with old and quaint roofed houses, to the famous Pontenezen Barracks some four miles from the docks. The barracks, interesting relics of Napoleon's sturdy soldiers, were there it is true, but our portion of the rest camp, as it had been called in orders, were fields in which we planted the humble flop. Fields are all very well but some of these were practically under water and all were a sea of mud. Every stick of firewood and pound of food was carried by hand from the commissary. All of these things are but an ordinary part of a soldier's existence to be sure, but it did grate later to read an inspired article in an American newspaper lauding the efficiency of the camp authorities for leasing the fields for our camp that same day, so when the tired and hungry troops arrived they found their camp ready and a smoking hot meal awaiting them.

Alvan Morgan poses before an American flag on the eve of his overseas deployment. *Courtesy Delaware Military Heritage and Education Foundation.*

The Pioneers pitched their shelter tents. The weather was continually rainy. The barracks used as the quartermaster depot were constructed by Napoleon as preparation for the invasion of England. On September 14, barely a week later, the unit transshipped by rail on a three-day journey through the lovely French farm country with the little white villages glistening among the trees. It was then that the men learned the true meaning of "Hommes 40, Chevaux 8" as forty men crowded into the boxcars. They enjoyed the scenery by day but struggled all night for a place to sleep. The soldiers passed through town after town, stopping only every ten to twelve hours to stretch their cramped limbs. They passed through historic locales such as Versailles and Tours and even caught a glimpse of the Eiffel Tower as they were on the outskirts of Paris. The train turned south, causing speculation that they were bound for Italy. The Pioneers passed through some of the most scenic parts of France until finally stopping at a village called Foulain, Department Haute-Marne. The place was described in Sergeant Summers' diary:

> *The large towns and cities resemble the large towns and cities in the U.S.A. excepting there are no frame buildings, everything is stone in which the country abounds. In the rural districts the people do not live on the farms, but a big beautiful church is built and all the inhabitants of the neighborhood build their houses around the church. The houses and barns are combined and built as one building composed entirely of stone. You open the kitchen door and enter right into the stable where the horse, cattle and sheep are housed along with an occasional few fowl such as geese, ducks, chickens and guineas. The people take care of their stock, you never see an animal unless it is rolling in fat. The people cultivate the neighboring ground raising considerable rye, potatoes, sugar beets, rutabagas, and hay. Very little corn being raised as the weather is too cool and wet to raise it profitably. The people are great wine drinkers, they drink it for breakfast, dinner and supper, just as we drink coffee.*

The Pioneers pitched their shelter tents in a garden spot of green grass. Two young officers, Lieutenant William Berl and Lieutenant Harry Van Sciver, who both spoke French, were instrumental in helping the regiment communicate among the French authorities. The encampment was alongside the Seine-Marne Canal, so for the first time in two weeks, the men had the opportunity for a cold freshwater bath and took full advantage of their circumstances. All was dull and uneventful until the following Sunday, September 22, when the mademoiselles in the surrounding neighborhood paid a visit, which cheered the boys greatly. While the French were generally welcoming and pleasant, a soldier noted that whenever Americans were present, the price of wine and champagne seemed to instantly escalate. The favorite times for doughboys were mail call and payday. Letters from friends, family and loved ones were morale boosters, and failure to get a letter from home would cast a pall of gloom. The men were paid in French francs. A black organization arrived at this encampment a few days after the arrival of the Fifty-ninth. When one of their party also bathed in the canal, a man was lost to drowning in the cold water when he tried to swim across the canal.

While at Foulain, the Fifty-ninth lost to disease two men, who fell victim within a few days. The Spanish influenza, which had begun in the spring in the training camps, would emerge in the autumn and winter with even more strength.

A gas mask drill at the Fifty-ninth Pioneer Infantry Regiment camp. *Courtesy Marie Ferguson.*

At Foulain, the regiment was trained in gas defense. The French greeted the mostly green soldiers of the American Expeditionary Force with joy. France and Britain were militarily and spiritually spent after three years of deadlock. Their losses had been catastrophic. The first Americans troops to parade down Parisian boulevards were greeted by crying and cheering Frenchmen who threw flowers and kisses at the troops. On July 4, 1917, Paris celebrated American Independence Day. A U.S. battalion marched to the Picpus Cemetery, where several speeches were made at Lafayette's tomb. Colonel Charles E. Stanton, an aide to the American commander general John J. Pershing, would declare, "Lafayette, we are here!"

The headquarters company included the famous Fifty-ninth Pioneer Infantry Band, at the top of the list of bands representing the Second Army, as well as cooks, mechanics, buglers and one horse-shoer. The Fifty-ninth Pioneer Infantry Band gained fame throughout the area as one of the best. When the *Leviathan* anchored at Brest on September 7, 1918, the band remained on board playing during the time it took to coal the ship. Debarkation was completed on September 9, and the band proceeded through Brest to Pontanezen Barracks, performing a number of concerts to relieve the monotony and the hardships among the men. Its music library was lost in transit, but finally replaced in Sorcy, where it entertained the troops. On Christmas Day 1918, trucks took the band to Boucq to entertain the Third Battalion. The band also performed at Toul for Second Army Headquarters and at numerous base hospitals nearby. Toul was also the primary base of the United States Air Service during World War I. After the Fifty-Ninth Band's selection as the best band in a competition held by Second Army, it was assigned to the French Riviera, a leave area, to perform at Monte Carlo for veterans on leave from the front. According to the wartime diary of veteran Anthony Summers:

> *The men work all day and during the evening visit the "soda water" resorts, or gather around for a card party, or play a visit to the Y.M.C.A. hut to play a game of dominoes, write a letter, or listen to the beautiful strains of* Joan of Arc, *played by the world famous 59th Pioneer Infantry Band.*

The Fifty-ninth remained an independent unit and was not merged with any division until the formation of field armies in France. Because of the urgent need for troops at the front, the units of the Fifty-ninth were almost immediately assigned to duty at various points in the First Army's zone in the Meuse-Argonne area. The pressing needs of war meant that the regiment would be broken into components once more.

The enemy was already on the defensive as American forces worked their way up to full strength. On September 26, the Americans began their strike toward the vital rail link at Sedan in the south; British and Belgian divisions drove toward Ghent (Belgium) on the twenty-seventh, and then British and French armies attacked across northern France on the twenty-eighth. The scale of the overall offensive, bolstered by the fresh U.S. troops, signaled renewed vigor among the Allies and sharply dimmed German hopes for victory. The Meuse-Argonne offensive, shared by the U.S. forces with the French Fourth Army on the left, was the biggest operation and victory of the American Expeditionary Force (AEF) in World War I. The bulk of the AEF had not gone into action until 1918. It would be a forty-seven-day offensive, employing twenty-two American Divisions, with 750,000 men, and over four

CROIX ROUGE

BELGIUM

LUXEMBOURG

STENAY

LONGWY

REHON

LONGUYON

BUZANCY

VOUZIERS

DUN

BILLY
MANGIENNES

GRANDPRE

ARGONNE

DAMVILLERS

CIEROES GERCOURT
SEPTSARGES
BRABANT
AZANNES
BETHINCOURT

ABRI DE CROCHET VARENNES
ESNES

BATTLE LINE NOV 7 1918

VALLEROY
CONFLANS

BATTLE LINE JULY 18 1918

APREMONT DOMBASLE
VERDUN

METZ

CLERMONT EN ARGONNE
LES ISLETTES SOUHESME LA GRANDE
STE MENEHOULD

LORRAINE

MOSELLE R.

M E U S E

VIEVILLE SOUS-LES-COTES
VIGNEULLES

TRIAUCOURT

THIAUCOURT

HEUDICOURT BOUILLONVILLE FEY EN HAYE
BUXIERES PANNES EUVEZIN
WOINVILLE CHARERAIS REGNIEVILLE
STMIHIEL LIRONVILLE MONTAUVILLE

VARNEVILLE FLIREY SEICHEPREY
AMPREMONT OERNECOURT
BROUSSEY GROSROUVRES
RAULECOURT

GRISCOURT BELLEVILLE
OEZONCOURT
MARBACHE

M E U R T H E

HEILTZ LE-MAURUPT

BAR-LE-DUC

LEROUVILLE
COMMERCY BOUCQ
ST MARINS
LANEUVILLE SORCY TRONDES
S/MEUSE

KOSHES-EN-HAYE
ANFILLY
LIVERDUN

E T M O S E L L E
TOUL NANCY

VOID

CHAUDNEY

A map of the areas in which the Fifty-ninth Pioneer Infantry served in France. *Courtesy Delaware Military Heritage and Education Foundation.*

hundred heavy guns in a pivotal attack that smashed the Hindenburg line on the western front and forced the imperial German command to sue for armistice. It was the largest military operation yet seen in American history and the deadliest of the war.

Most of the Fifty-ninth Regiment was sent toward the front from Foulain on September 27 during the Meuse-Argonne offensive. Its war had begun in earnest. It would be relatively brief, as the armistice was only some six weeks in the future.

The scene that greeted the Pioneers, for all its terrors, was a grandiose one. After the fog had lifted, it was clear autumn weather. The Pioneer's official history describes machine guns and rifles rattling on every side as the troops went forward over the almost impassable terrain, scarred by years of warfare.

Overhead, our aeroplanes were engaged in constant combat with the Huns, swirling about like a cluster of autumn leaves in the wind. Here and there behind us a daring enemy aviator worked his too often repeated trick of destroying an observation balloon and racing for his own lines under a storm of fire. The roads were congested with miles and miles of traffic troops, ambulances, trucks, wagons, tanks and later tractors; guns and caissons stretched in endless lines, sometimes motionless for hours as some blockage was cleared away. Prisoners filtered through in bodies of twenty to two hundred, occasionally carrying wounded Americans. Haughty Prussian officers with gold monocles, hard, sulky-looking soldiers, frightened Slavs

A walking wounded captive is escorted behind the lines to an aid station.
Courtesy Library of Congress.

with rosaries prominently displayed as if to appeal to the feelings of their captors and many boys certainly under sixteen years of age who in happier times would have been romping to school but now clumping along with hanging heads in their green uniforms, round hats and leather boots.

On October 10, 1918, when the Second Army was formed, regimental headquarters and the First and Second Battalions were assigned to it, with the Third Battalion remaining with the First Army. The Fifty-ninth was split up, with different companies detailed to separate points. The various tasks assigned to the units included road building and maintenance, factory operation, general construction, camouflage, waterworks, treatment plants, pipeline repair and railroad construction and operation. Much of this work was done under continual air raids and shellfire, including gas shells.

This service is commemorated on the colors of the present-day Delaware National Guard units descended from the Fifty-ninth by the rainbow-hued battle streamer for the Meuse-Argonne offensive. The men of the Fifty-ninth were frequently moved hither and yon, sometimes by rail, sometimes by truck and very often by foot and, when in the combat zone, often at night. A Pioneer describes his experiences:

Promptly at 1500, we moved out of the woods and took the road under a dark and threatening sky. The marching was under, as always, a heavy pack and equipment, including entrenching tools, rifles and a hundred rounds of ammunition and steel helmets, and the formation a column of twos. The ground showed everywhere traces of severe fighting, dead men and animals were passed along the road and a stormy atmospheric condition added gloom to the tragic picture. An early darkness fell, yet slightly to the left ahead the sky seemed on fire along the skyline owing to a peculiar sunset effect. This died out after a time and we were marching through absolute darkness in utter silence, seeing but faintly the road ahead by fitful flashes in the sky. Eerie whistling noises sounded overhead from unseen missiles in action all around in the darkness. After some hours march through total darkness the ghostly indistinct outlines of the shattered walls of the outskirts of the city crept like gray inky shadows out of the blackness and the way was picked through the debris-piled streets, between jagged shadowy walls that once were buildings, in darkness so intense that the man ahead could not be seen more than five feet away. This place was at intervals heavily shelled, yet during the time that we passed through there was nothing but blackness and a silence that was oppressive. Shortly after the regiment had passed through, however, a heavy shelling of the city occurred from German batteries that had accurate range. When this took place our company was lying on the ground along a fringe of trees near the city's edge, so we were ordered behind an embankment at the edge of a woods a quarter of a mile away where we remained through the night, taking-cover in the woods.

Combat service approached the limits of some men's endurance. Artillery barrages drove some men mad. The men burrowed into their trenches or dugouts only to re-roil the mud. Their bunkmates were the rats. The soldiers suffered from lice (cooties) and forced them to disrobe at every opportunity in order to run fingernails down the seams of their uniforms to dislodge the disagreeable creatures. "We can hear the cannons roaring on the front lines, as we are only about 20 miles from St. Mihiel and we see the aeroplanes fly overhead so much that we will have sprained necks by the time we return," wrote Sergeant Summers. On November 3, he added:

Pop returned and reiterated all about his wondrous trip (to the front). He had some hair-breadth escapes and brought back as a memento three Boche helmets, dozens of buttons, and a few pfennigs which he had procured from the enemy. Told all about the Metz front where he was compelled to seek shelter in a protected dug-out. Also visited the Argonne Forests where the gas gongs sounded and all were compelled to resort to their old comrade the gas mask. He said the firing was intense from the big guns. Also stated that if a man lived at the front of them very long he would never again become civilized. During the week, we have had an air raid almost every night and the sky would be lighted up by the bursting shells from the anti-aircraft guns close by.

Despite these hardships the fighting spirit of the men endured. On October 23, men of the Supply Company received a mailbag, took a walk to the YMCA for some writing paper, and drew books from the library. They returned and began to read their books... An explosion was heard close by. The men rushed out to see what was coming off, and saw an enemy aeroplane dropping bombs close by, and saw the bombs explode, tearing up earth all around them. Then they heard the anti-aircraft guns belch forth and explode its golden stars in the bright moonlit sky. Then a machine gun opened fire in the air, which was recognized to be an allied aircraft, it was then that the Frenchmen crawled out of their shell-proof bunkers and exclaimed "Boche finis!"

On Nov. 8, 40 skilled mechanics were sent to Grosrouvres for construction work. The remainder procured about 100 German prisoners to clean up the town. They worked and grunted all afternoon under the vigilant eyes of our guard who, with bayonets fixed and rifles loaded had all they could do to keep the French populace calm and away from them…

It is very interesting to watch the fair sex as a body of prisoners pass. They argue with one another and shake their fists at their former antagonists who in reply only smile that German smile of defiance. The prisoners are mostly boys, who do not look to be over 15 to 16 years of age at most.

November 1918 brought cool dry clement and pleasantly sunny weather with cool frosty nights. The men were given their winter uniforms and new equipment. Encouraging news came that Turkey had signed peace terms and Austria was in a state of revolt. The Italians were advancing to the German border as well. The Pioneers were entertained in the evening by the buzz of machinery running smoothly in the air, then you would hear a hit and miss sound like a four cylinder auto running on three cylinders, and would recognize this to be a bombing plane, then the searchlights would locate the machine, and the sky would be lighted up with bursting shells from our anti-aircraft guns…

The local townspeople were very much agitated about news that Germany was seeking a peace. The Frenchmen would stand up to you and discuss things in his own language for an hour at a time, and all you have to say is "oui, oui" or "compree" and guess what he was saying.

Finally on Monday, November 11, 1918, Germany signed the armistice, ending the war. Church bells tolled incessantly, guns were fired into the air and flags were flying from every house and public building, the French tricolor and the Stars and Stripes side by side.

Postwar Garrison

The exhausted doughboys of the American Expeditionary Force climbed from their muddy trenches, lit warming fires and reflected on the high cost of their victory. In two hundred days of combat, 50,280 men died and over 200,000 were wounded.

With the stability of peace, the Pioneers began to improve their lot somewhat with the arrival of barrack stoves to warm their quarters as the cold of winter approached. On November 17, the men observed the Sabbath by washing themselves and their clothing. The men of the supply

In a break from their duties, soldiers enjoy the YMCA library. *Courtesy Library of Congress.*

company rode army bicycles three kilometers to the nearby town of Void and observed German prisoners constructing barracks and auxiliary buildings. The soldiers were permitted to write home and, for the first time, accurately report their actual whereabouts versus the usual "somewhere in France." The peacetime routine began to rapidly reassert itself.

Daniel Slack wrote on November 16:

> *We are having pretty cool weather over here now. And this is not such a bad country over here? But the old U.S.A. has got them all beat. And we are in a German dug out now, and there is a good many hills and mountains where we are at now, and I will tell you all about this country when I get back, if I ever get back, for I can tell you better than I can write about it, for I'm too lazy to write.*

The regiment was slowly reassembled. Christmas celebrations were held; every man in the regiment was presented with a souvenir of France, and every mess was supplied with a ration of either turkey or goose. The men slept in until

9:00 a.m. after the Christmas Eve revelries. The men fell in at 2:00 p.m. and marched to the square, where a Christmas tree had been erected next to the YMCA hut. The men sang "The Star-Spangled Banner" accompanied by the band, followed by about one hundred French children singing "The Marseilles." Then each child was presented with a small token. Speeches were made by Colonel Reed, Chaplain Davis and Major LaFevre. The men dined at 4:30 p.m. Boxing was the Christmas entertainment, and eight bouts of three rounds each were held. The inhabitants of the towns where the Fifty-ninth Infantry were billeted remembered the Christmas of 1918 for a long time.

An ammunition dump, part of the postwar salvage stock, managed by the Fifty-ninth Pioneers. *Courtesy Marie Ferguson.*

After the armistice, the units of the Fifty-ninth were assigned to duty salvaging German war materiel, ordnance demolition and operation of quartermaster and ordnance depots. The casualties were not at an end however. Tragically, on January 22, 1919, Wilmington soldiers Thomas Davis, Harvey Hadley, Howard Johnson and John Chandler and three other regiment soldiers from Company I were killed in a mine explosion in Rehon, near Toul, France. During the actual hostilities, none of the regiment men were killed in action, even though they were frequently under shell fire during the drive in the Argonne Forest. However, several Pioneer soldiers did perish as a result of disease.

A list of the articles the Pioneers were to salvage would fill a catalogue. Chiefly, they had to collect Allied and enemy weapons and cannon, web and leather equipment, clothing and blankets, rolling stock and aviation and electrical and engineering equipment. It was a gigantic task and did not near completion until the first week in March, when more than three thousand

French carloads had been shipped. For some weeks, truck transportation was scarce and work was slow, consisting largely of getting material to roadsides.

Despite the hardships and the heavy work of salvage and demolition, there were compensating benefits. The men were issued passes and took full advantage of the opportunity to see the sights and enjoy the French culture. Sergeant Albert Summers's letters record visits to the birthplace of Joan of Arc at Demremy in the Vosges in January. In March, he was granted a pass to visit Paris.

Summers went on to describe a brief sightseeing expedition in January 1919 to Montsec:

> We started out walking towards St. Mihiel but had only gone three kilometers viewing the artillery emplacements along the narrow gauge and the machine gun nests in the tree tops, when one of our Fords came along and we drove on up to where the Headquarters of our 2nd battalion is located in Rolencourt, about eight kilometers from Boucq. We then decided to visit that famous slaughter house of Montsec. So we drove on through four or five has been towns, but are now nothing but masses of ruins, not a single room being left in the towns. The picture is indescribable. All along the road are shell holes both great and small, for it was here that some of the most stubborn fighting in the war was pulled off. Montsec is about 15 kilometers from here and it was this mount that the Germans occupied until September, 1918. It is an isolated spot of the Vosges Range. The Germans had erected at the foot of same a large iron cross and had built some fine concrete dugouts. A continuous tunnel runs around the mountain near the peak, but as the wire had been disconnected and parts of the tunnel caved in, we could only find our way around by the aid of a searchlight. The top is bare of trees from the continual artillery fire. From the top of this mount Metz can be seen in the distance. The French tried to rush this place and in so doing lost 36,000 men in 24 hours. When the Americans took it in September 1918, they lost 35 men. With the loss of Montsec, the St. Mihiel sector withered away, and the Boche was kept on the run. After walking all over the mount we returned to our machine and returned to our roosting place in time to sign the pay-roll.

Meanwhile, the ruined Argonne was re-clothing itself in the vestments of spring. Beside the thousands of little crosses that marked the graves of brave American soldiers, there sprang up the *pierce-niege* (snow drop), and the fields bloomed with the ever-present cocou (a species of yellow primrose).

The rains were less frequent, and there were many days of such beautiful weather that the men who had come to the conclusion that there was no sun in France changed their minds. On March 21, 1919, the Fifty-ninth Pioneer Infantry was transferred from the Second Army to the Advance Section, Service of Supply. By now, all the Pioneers were sick and tired of France and the dull routine of garrison duty. Rumors circulated among the disheartened troops that they would soon ship home. Their hopes of early embarkation were repeatedly dashed. The regiment finally reunited at LeMans on May 25. The soldiers camped about two kilometers from town in British hospital tents in a little green apple orchard. It appeared that they were sidetracked by the inefficiencies of military bureaucracy without any idea when they might return to Hoboken. According to Sergeant Summers, "Everyone was trying to make the best of it, but it was very disheartening when one thinks one is homeward bound."

At last, they entrained for Brest on June 14, where they were physically examined and reequipped. They decamped from Camp Pontanegen, Brest on July 27 and reboarded the *Leviathan*. On June 29, 1919, the headquarter company of the Fifty-ninth sailed from Brest, arriving at Hoboken on July 5.

Other units sailed separately during the month. In July, the men of the regiment were discharged at Camp Dix. The 1,500 Delawareans, and many of the men from New Jersey and New York who served with the outfit, came home to the most rousing parade and civic reception Wilmington had ever seen.

The following poem by an unknown author neatly summarizes the experience of the Fifty-ninth during the Great War:

"The Pioneers"

We read about the doughboys and their valor, which is true,
And of the gallant part they played for the old Red, White and Blue:
We read about the HFA and their ever-roaring guns,
Also the heavy part they played in blowing up the Huns;
The Infantry, the Cavalry, the hardy Engineers,
But we never read a single word about
The Pioneers.
They slept in pup tents in the cold and worked in mud and mire,
They filled up shell holes in the roads, 'most always under fire;
Far o'er the lines the scout plane goes, directing the barrage,
Just as zero hour draws nigh, or just before the charge.

As o'er the top the doughboy goes, to put the Hun to tears,
But who went out and cut the wire?
The Husky Pioneers.
They buried beaucoup horses and carried beaucoup shells.
From every dump on every front, the kind of work that tells.
A heavy pack on every back, on every track in France,
They never wore the Croix de Guerre—
They never had a chance.
And as the heavy trucks rolled by, they worked to calm their fears.
Who made the rocky roads so smooth?
The same old Pioneers.
Each branch deserves much credit, and I like to read their praise,
We helped them all, both great and small, in many different ways;
The Shock Troops and brave Marines, the Ammunition Train,
The Signal Corps, the Tank Corps, and the Observation Plane.
The War is won, the work is done, so here's three hearty cheers,
For the outfit that I soldiered with,
The good old Pioneers. (One of Them)

Although the Delaware National Guard represented the largest single contingent of soldiers who served during World War I, it is by no means the only organization with Delaware soldiers. Following are some other representative samples of letters and reminisces from others who served, telling different facets of the story.

THE HODGSON SIBLINGS

Mary Hodgson trained as a registered nurse and, as a Red Cross volunteer, was sent to France before the United States entered the war. She was based at a Red Cross hospital in La Treport tending to soldiers and civilians wounded during the conflict. Mary wrote in March 1918:

> *We have some boys that have been badly blistered with mustard gas, coughing with lungs filled up with fluid. We can help some of them, but too many times all we can do is dope the pain while they cough horribly and pray for release. My heart is heavy with the cruelty of poison gas, which lasts several days after an attack has taken place. Everything is broken as*

we have never seen on such a scale. But where there is any chance at all, we try to save the poor souls wounded from either army, or the innocent local farmers and their families.

Mary stayed on in France for five months after the war ended, returning to Delaware in March 1919. Her brother Edward was in France as well but never crossed paths with his sister Mary. After basic training, Edward spent five days crossing the Atlantic on a troop ship to Brest. In a letter dated October 18, 1918, he wrote:

I've had all kinds of jobs over here. Filling shell holes, breaking rock, shoveling sand, mending roads, carrying lumber, piling baled hay (for protective walls) and everything else. I have seen some nurses with their gum boots on, but I haven't seen Mary among them.

Less than two weeks later, Private Hodgson joined thousands of other soldiers who fell victim to the influenza sweeping the continent. He survived the disease but had not realized the war was over until some time after the armistice, when he was finally well enough to read and write again.

BROTHERS IN ARMS

Walter Willoughby Josephs and Howard W. Josephs were brothers born in Philadelphia and raised with three sisters in Seaford and Smyrna, Delaware. Both joined the military as marines, both serving in France and surviving the conflict.

Lieutenant Walter Willoughby Josephs

Walter Willoughby Josephs graduated from Smyrna High School and Delaware College, where he played varsity football. His degree was in mechanical engineering. While working as an engineer for the DuPont Powder Company, he attended classes at the Academy of Fine Arts in Philadelphia.

When America entered the war, Walter enrolled at the Delaware Aeronautical Company and learned to pilot flying boats. After graduation, he entered the navy, assigned to Key West Naval Air Station but transferred to the First

Marine Aviation Force. Flying boats were not to his liking. The First Marine deployed to France in July 1918. Because the force did not have enough aircraft of its own, in September, Josephs was transferred to the Third French Military Aircraft Squadron, flying a Caproni bomber with an aerial gunner. Later, he flew an American Liberty–powered DeHaviland two-seat bomber.

The squadron flew fourteen raids during the balance of the war, doing considerable damage and bringing back useful intelligence on the Flanders

A self-portrait of Lieutenant Walter Willoughby Josephs with his bomber. *Courtesy Marjorie Vaughn.*

front. A French regiment was cut off from its own lines near Stadenberg, and the marine pilots loaded up their craft with food and essentials and successfully air dropped 2,600 pounds of supplies to the beleaguered French over a period of two days. The marine airmen had to fly low and slow to accomplish this mission during heavy ground fire until the unit was successfully extricated.

The unit was transferred to Norfolk, Virginia, arriving on December 21, 1918. Josephs was mustered out in January 1919. He returned to France after the war to study art in 1922. He opened a studio in Philadelphia, specializing in portraits and murals. He did return to duty status in December 1941, serving at Miramar Air Station for the duration of World War II, retiring as a major in 1946. He taught art in San Diego and did portraits until his death in 1973.

Private Howard W. Josephs

Howard W. Josephs reported for duty as a recruit on April 25, 1917, one of seventy-two men from Delaware who enlisted in the Marine Corps from 1917 to 1918. Private Josephs deployed to France on June 14, 1917, with the Fifty-fifth Company, Fifth Regiment, Fourth Brigade, Second Marine Division American Expeditionary Forces, assigned to the Army Fourth Infantry Division. He saw action at Château-Thierry and the Battle of Belleau Woods in June 1918, where he was wounded. He recovered after a hospital stay.

On July 19, while fighting in Vierzy, Howard continued to operate his automatic weapon even though his two helpers were both wounded. There were nineteen marine fatalities during this action.

In September, Howard was once again in the thick of the action at the St. Mihiel salient. In October, he was in the Champagne Sector and the Battle of Blanc Mont Ridge as part of the Meuse-Argonne offensive. In November, he was promoted to corporal. After the armistice, he marched toward the Rhine via Belgium and Luxembourg following the evacuation of the German army. The Fifth Regiment remained in garrison as an occupying army until August when it was deployed home and mustered out on August 13.

Howard was awarded the Croix de Guerre with palm for his actions at Vierzy. His Fifth Regiment was awarded the Fourragere. The Marine Fifth and Sixth Regiments were the only American regiments in the

AEF to receive three Croix de Guerre citations. These two regiments were awarded the Fourragere and Croix de Guerre with two palms and a Silver Gilt Star. In addition, Howard was awarded two battle stars for his bravery in battle.

FRANK LEWIS OF DOVER ESCAPES HUN SHELLS

An October 26, 1918 letter to Mr. and Mrs. Robert H. Lewis read:

My Dear Father and All:

Since I am taking this day off I'll drop a line. I am sitting in my dugout keeping a home made stove going. I took a five gallon gasoline can cut a door and a pipe hole in it, so this is our stove. Our dugout is small but can make out very well. I am about five miles back from the front line trenches. The three inch guns are back of me and near me are six inch shell guns so we are well entertained day and night. I arrived here three days ago and have already seen three battles and been bombarded twice. We arrived at night, pitched our tents on the side of a hill, went to bed. All through the night old Fritz shells were whizzing over our heads and landing in the valley just beyond. The following day the sky was full of German planes. Battles took place all day long.

When our days work was through and we returned to our tents, Fritz opened up, six landed on top of our hill, not a hundred yards away, about six to the right of us, and about the same distance, we still stood there thinking Fritz still did not have our range. About this time one landed a little this side of the high top and one landed south of us across the little valley. Now is when the running started, some ran into the wire entanglements, which are still standing, some fell over tents, some crawling into shell holes, and some ran for the already occupied dugouts. I thought I was running, but about seven fellows passed me, so I thought I had better drop my blankets and speed up, which I did, and safety was reached. Very little damage was done, nothing worth speaking of for war times.

We need no moving pictures to entertain us over here. The air battles are the most interesting and exciting part of war to witness. They take place within sight of the naked eye. Aviators bring us papers each day they fly over and drop them. From the time we left school until the day we arrived at this place was just five weeks. We are riding part of the time, walking part of the time, and lost half of the time such a time we had. Most of the nights we slept in freight cars and stole what we ate. We now have our packs down to almost nothing, what we have on our backs, a towel, a few extra socks, few old letters, gun, and bullets. Some one stole my razor and toilet articles so I am cutting my beard with a pair of little scissors. I could tell you lots of things, but what's the use of doing it now, when I get home I can entertain you by the hour with truth and not imaginary stories. I must chop some wood for my stove as the fire is low. This is not like home, but it's far better than I've had the past five weeks so of course, I am enjoying it. Don't worry over me for I am coming home with the boys when this is all over.

Just lots of love for you all.
FRANK LEWIS

DONALD HORSEY IN LAST HUN BATTLE

Horsey wrote a letter to his mother from Biergelem, Belgium, on November 13, 1918:

Dearest Mother:

I look forward to writing this letter since I have plenty of time and a great many good things to tell you. Of course you have read of the armistice and know more about it, perhaps [more] *than we do as we get no papers here. But thank God we know the most important thing of all, that the fighting has stopped and for that every soldier is grateful. Were I at any place to cable you I should for I know you would be very happy to feel that I am well and happy. This will relieve you of any anxiety that you may have as to my whereabouts at least.*

The tables have turned now and it is I who am uneasy as to how you all are. Yesterday I ran into Lofland Jones and he told me of the Spanish Influenza. Since I have not heard from you. I wonder if you have been troubled with it at home? Tell me when you write. I was sorry to hear of Reynold Clough's death. Lofland gave me a Delaware State News *and you can bet I was happy to see some familiar names etc., the first home news since I left, September 9th. Turning back to October 30th about four o'clock in the afternoon, we started to the front. About fifteen miles away. When we had gotten about ten miles a message came up with the order to issue 100 rounds of ammunition to each man. We knew what that meant—fight. At ten that night we reached our destination just behind the lines. That night we spent in an open field in spite of heavy shelling and gas.*

Before day we lost about fifteen men, two of whom had been killed by shrapnel in their sleep. At 5:30 the next morning we went "over the top." I shall never forget the experience and it is only through the mercy of God that I am here to tell about it.

Starting out with eighty men in the company and forty five in my platoon we had left after the first ten minutes about half that number, the others had either been killed or wounded. One shell exploded in the midst of one of my combat groups and put out eight men. How any of us lived through such shelling, I can't say. It was not due to any clever maneuvering of ours for we had to wade right through it and take what came. During the first five minutes our company commander was gassed and that left me in command. I almost felt like a murderer for I realized how incompetent I was. The least misstep would have meant the life of practically all of us, and knowing this I surely felt sorry for the men. But we got along pretty well some way, and after the conditions it is remarkable that any are still left. At the end of the first day I had 27 men left in the company. Later, others showed up who were lost and went back with the wounded. After sleeping in a shell hole all night we went over the top again the following morning at 6 o'clock. That day was not so bad and we lost fewer men. During the day we advanced about six miles. Again we slept in shell holes, that is we stayed in them, but got little rest because of the heavy shelling. Sixteen of my men were quartered in a barn where a shell made a direct hit, causing practically the whole thing to fall over. For hours the men were crushed under the ruins and despite vigorous work one died before we could free him. All were injured but only one seriously. It was remarkable that any of them lived. For three days we stayed in our little holes, sometimes eating and sometimes not, until finally we were relieved.

The major sent me out with eight men the day we were relieved to pick out the route. When we had accomplished our mission, a sergeant and I went to a little house to get a bite to eat and there await the arrival of the battalion. As we sat there eating eggs and bread they played "America" on the old graphaphone, and not even "Ole Virginny" could have sounded sweeter. The last tone had hardly died out when the town was bombed by "Terry Planes," and it was very unpleasant there for awhile.

We hiked about ten miles that night and slept in a barn. Believe me, it was cold. The next morning our hike was continued in a driving rain to Thielt. Here we billeted and for the first time in quite a period I slept in a bed. The officers had billets with the citizens of the town. Three machine gun officers

A hungry soldier enjoys a hot meal. *Courtesy Library of Congress.*

stayed with a lady who had previously had Prince Rupprecht as her guest, but an unwelcome one. He had left a short time before we arrived. There was a little child that who was born August 14, 1914. He had not seen his father, who had gone to war on August 6, 1914. Those are the things we run up against every day in this country. It is pitiful to see children living in such conditions. Those at home should be thankful, humble as they may be.

We stayed in Thielt three days and we expected to go to a rest camp from there, for we surely were deserving of it, but unexpectedly we were shot back into the line. I suppose you received my letter from there just before we left. For two days we hiked after leaving Thielt, and we expected to go over the top in a drive on Ghent on the fourth day, but at 2 a.m. on the second day we got orders to attack on the third day, November 9. We hiked the rest of the night and at 5 a.m. we attacked. As I told you in my last letter, I had been made intelligence officer of the battalion and hence my work was somewhat different this time. Though I liked my work very much in this scrap, it was rather a ticklish job. However, as you can see, I got there O.K. Again I can say, thank God for it was He was kind. The sergeant whom I had with me was killed and another of my men was shot by a machine gunner. It is a miracle that any of us escaped, for our objective was almost impregnable. All day we fought and maneuvered until finally at 1:30 in the morning we accomplished our mission, the crossing of the Escant River. Our regiment and the 146th, on our right, were the only ones to affect a crossing over the river during the war, so we feel rather proud.

At 3:00 a.m. we heard of the signing of the armistice. That was just before we crossed, but we were determined to get over so we went on. We didn't stop fighting until about 5 a.m. after that only shelling took place until 11 a.m. then all firing ceased. About 30 minutes before we had a man severely injured by shrapnel. In a nutshell mother, I have told you of some of our fighting. There are things which I shall never tell you about, and others I could not. If it were not all over, I should not write on this way, but I know you will not worry now. We have had a hard road to travel but God has been so good to me that I cannot grumble about my slight inconveniences when I see so much suffering around me every day.

Just now we are staying in a small village and the officers have quarters in a large convent here; we are very comfortable and the sisters can't do too much for us. The people in this country are so grateful for what America has done for them. They think the Red Cross is wonderful and speak of it often, saying it kept them from starving. They are quite different people from the French, and the boys seem to like them better because they understand us and appreciate us more. But don't think we don't like the French too I surely admire them. These people and their army; they are wonderful soldiers. There is a rumor that we are to go to Brussels from here. I should not be surprised, though I do not know yet. We are about twenty miles from there now. During the next few months we will probably roam about the country. Our movements will depend how soon peace comes. How long will it be before we start home no one can say, but several months at least. Don't look for me too soon. We must be grateful in the thought that it will be sometime.

I am looking forward to some mail and surely hope it comes ere long. Continue to write for we will be here some time and I will be somewhat lonesome at times. Give my love to all those at home. It will be a happy day for me when I can see you all again. Take care of yourselves and don't worry about me. I am well and O.K. in every way.

With all love to everyone, I am, as always,
Your loving son,
DON
C.C. 147th Infantry
A.P.A. 763, A.E.F. Belgium

6

AMONG THE CLOUDS

THE WAR IN THE AIR, OVER THERE

Delawareans served at sea and in the trenches as they had since the founding of the nation. The Great War brought a new dimension to warfare as aircraft evolved into weapons of war.

DELAWARE AERONAUTICAL COMPANY

In the spring of 1917, Pierre S. du Pont, Irénée du Pont and John J. Raskob created a flying school in Claymont, Delaware, to train pilots. All three were executives of the DuPont Powder Company, and they called their school the Delaware Aeronautical Company. They each contributed $20,000 to fund the school's objective of training pilots for government air service.

They hired Harry Atwood on April 14, 1917, just a dozen days after the declaration of war by President Wilson. Atwood had flown a Wright Model B 1,300 miles from St. Louis to New York in twelve days. He had designed a new aircraft engine in Williamsport, Pennsylvania, and tested it on a flying boat in the Susquehanna River in 1916. He was charged with developing the school curriculum. Atwood was a detail-oriented man who documented weekly reports to the directors outlining specific accomplishments and projections. He accounted for every penny spent.

A recruiting poster reads, "Join the Air Service, Learn and Earn." *Courtesy Library of Congress.*

The school was located on a portion of the Raskob estate in Claymont, Delaware, along the Delaware River. A landing field was cleared, and three hangars were constructed, along with a weather station. The adjacent river permitted seaplane operations. A Curtis JN-4B, often called a "Jenny," was ordered in May, along with spare parts. On a separate order, two Thomas flying boats were sent for.

On May 31, 1917, two instructors made the maiden test flight from the field in the Jenny. They surveyed the local flying area for alternate landing sites in case of a flying emergency. They attracted considerable attention from spectators when they passed over Wilmington at about one thousand feet.

By June 12, the initial class of twenty-one students had been enrolled. They were mostly college boys who had already applied and been accepted into the U.S. Aviation Corps. Most graduates signed on as naval aviators, although some chose the Army Air Service.

The students were cloistered at the field in Spartan conditions, with stern discipline regarding drinking and smoking on the premises. No visitors were allowed either. Their day was from 5:00 a.m. to sundown. Nevertheless, the school attracted some three hundred applicants. Few were chosen due to space and training personnel limitations.

The du Ponts and Raskob charged nothing to take the course, viewing it as their patriotic responsibility to provide aviators to defend their country.

The flying season ended on November 30, when the students of the school held a dinner at the Hotel DuPont in honor of the founders.

On May 21, 1918, the school participated in a patriotic Red Cross parade in Wilmington by allowing one of its airplanes to be trailered through the procession. This was the first opportunity for the local populace to see one of the airplanes close up.

On July 18, 1918, the directors announced the school would not open for the coming flying season. Government flying schools had finally caught up with demand, and the war was coming to an end. The equipment was donated to the School for Airplane Mechanics in New York. The Delaware Aeronautical Company had created the very first flight school in Delaware as well as the first operational flying field.

The story of Delaware's contribution to the air war is necessarily individual and episodic. One can get only a glimpse of the reality as told through the story of its aviators, whose stories are often tragedies. Following are representative samples.

Allen Oakley Smith

Allen Oakley Smith was killed by fall during a flight near Claymont, Delaware, on July 21, 1917. Smith was a Yale graduate. An arborist and forester before the war, he was the head gardener in the employ of John J. Raskob, treasurer of the DuPont Powder Company. On an unauthorized solo flight over the Delaware River, his machine was observed to be unsteady and wavering at a height of about one thousand feet. It suddenly fell and descended rapidly to the river, killing its pilot.

Lieutenant James Allison O'Daniel

James Allison "Al" O'Daniel was born on October 4, 1895, in Newark, Delaware, the son of James and Nora Wilson O'Daniel. At the time of his birth, his parents lived at 315 East Main Street with Mr. and Mrs. James Alexander Wilson, his maternal grandparents.

In 1914, O'Daniel entered Delaware College, now the University of Delaware. In July, he enlisted in Company E of the Delaware National Guard. He served on the Mexican border for seven months as a member of that unit in 1916 and 1917.

O'Daniel was back in college when the Delaware Regiment was organized. He was a member of the Delaware College class of 1918, having volunteered for service before graduating. Before going overseas, he had been living with his brother John Wilson O'Daniel and aunts Etta J. Wilson and Willie Nelson in their home at 313 East Main Street in Newark.

He enlisted in the Delaware regiment, which became part of the Fifty-ninth Pioneers, and was commissioned as a second lieutenant. He was assigned to Camp McClellan. In Austin, Texas, he attended the School of Military Aeronautics, graduating and reporting for duty overseas in July 1917. In his diary, O'Daniel describes his sea passage from New York with two other "Austin boys" on their way to France. The preponderance of the troops on board were from the First Aero Headquarters Regiment. They were picked from other regiments around the country, and every one of them spoke French. Many were French Canadians and, as a whole, highly educated.

O'Daniel drew watchman duty in the crow's nest—about one hundred feet above deck and reached by rope netting—for most of the voyage, a duty he enjoyed. He described a storm with winds of 120 miles per hour and waves crashing over the deck and then joked about six meals a day, "three in each direction," due to the seasickness. He lightly mocked the "nervous ones who sleep in their clothes" while in the "submarine zone." O'Daniel took comfort in the escort ships of destroyers and torpedo boats.

O'Daniel never mentioned the name of the vessel but says it had been torpedoed on three occasions. On one occasion it sank a sub in a running battle. On another it was hit, and the ship was abandoned but remained afloat and was brought into port under its own steam.

In Europe, O'Daniel attended two additional flying schools and was promoted to the rank of first lieutenant in the Signal Corps. In a letter dated April 13, 1918, to his grandmother, O'Daniel described landing in port (Brest) and a brief sojourn at the Pontenezen Barracks. The "people, that is the working class, all wear big wooden shoes while the women do all the work such as driving carts and in the stores. It is seldom that you see a real able bodied young man on the streets that is French."

He went on to describe "large and old cathedrals castles, chateaus, and many pretty villas along a river." And he adds a description of training in camp:

> We have to drill every day, stand reveille at 6:15 and drill 8:30 to 9:30; lectures from 10 to 11:30; drill 1:30 to 3:00; then we are through until 10 when everyone has to be in, or stay out all night. The lectures have been very interesting and instructive. One of them by an American F.A. captain who has been in the fighting and others by regular army captains.

In his letter, O'Daniel tells of an interesting chance encounter:

> They have a book here at the Y.M.C.A. which all new incoming officers sign. You put your name, rank, state, and town and date of arrival. I just now noticed the book and so I signed it. A few minutes later while I was writing here at the table a first lieutenant picked up the book and also signed it. He happened to see the name O'Daniel and that I was from Delaware, so he asked me if I knew a Lt. O'Daniel on the 11th Infantry. It so happened that he was in the same regiment, and did guard duty with Mike. [The nickname of O'Daniel's elder brother John Wilson O'Daniel.] He tells me the 11th regiment is over here someplace now. So you can bet I'm going to write to Kid at once.
>
> While looking through the names in the register I ran across about a dozen names of fellows who were with us in Austin but who sailed before

us. There were about 100 enlisted men of Company C, Delaware N.G. who arrived here yesterday under one of our lieutenants.

After August 1, 1918, Lieutenant O'Daniel was scheduled to go to an active combat air unit. First Lieutenant O'Daniel was attached to the Second Aviation Instruction Center. The Aviation Instruction Center in Tours, France, and the school of aerial photography were created by the famous photographer Edward Steichen, chief of the Photographic Section, Air Service.

The Observers School was opened in January 1918. The course given to observers was intended to cover all areas necessary to qualify the observer for front-line duty.

O'Daniel was a cameraman and observer on a reconnaissance flight. He died when his plane went down over France before the Battle of Château-Thierry on July 27, 1918. The accident was described by Chaplain B.R. Lacy in a letter to Rebecca Wilson, O'Daniel's grandmother:

Riding out past the aviation field I saw the plane take to the sky, and it passed over us so I could see the two occupants. We commented on our desire to go up some day and after were seated at a small restaurant on the lawn of our company noted that the motor was missing. A few minutes later a lieutenant at the table next to ours remarked that he had seen it descend abruptly to earth. Soon, a second plane left the field flying low in the direction of the place where the first plane had fallen. It was not long after it had returned that the ambulance rushed past and took both O'Daniel and his companion to the hospital. We mounted and rode to the scene of the accident the machine had sailed through some apple trees and struck the earth near a high bridge. There we found that your grandson had been killed and the pilot wounded. All of us were saddened beyond measure.

James Allison O'Daniel was the first Delawarean to be killed in action in World War I. O'Daniel was buried at Camp Coetquidan in Morbihan, France. He was the first to be interred at the little American cemetery there. Chaplain Lacy describes the military service:

First marched the band playing Chopin's wonderful piece of music. The body rested upon the caisson drawn by six large black artillery horses. A group of officers acted as pall bearers and another group including the commander of the camp followed, and then the rest of the Aviation Section. It then passed countless soldiers, they all came to attention and uncovered or saluted until the procession had passed. At the grove the ceremony was simple, but I think very impressive. As the body was being lowered the band played "Abide with Me" and over us flew one of the fellow officers of Lt. O'Daniel. As we laid the body away on the little hill so far from those who loved him most I could not help thinking of the lines so dear to one who is dear to me:

"There April o'er his lowly mound,
Shall shake the violets from her hair,
And June shall bid with fervent kiss,
The radiant roses blossom there,
While all around the drowsy bee
With droning hum shall come up and go,
And sweet South winds in pensive mood,
Singing funeral dirges soft and low."

After the war, O'Daniel was reburied at Oise-Aisne American Cemetery. Lieutenant James Allison O'Daniel's name is engraved on a bronze plaque in the center hall of the University of Delaware's Memorial Hall, and his name is inscribed in the *Book of Remembrance*, which has the names of those who died in the Great War from Delaware. This book is in a glass-covered case in the middle of the hall. Currently, members of the ROTC ceremoniously turn a page every day to display another name of one who died in the war.

Al was the younger brother of Lieutenant General "Iron Mike" John Wilson O'Daniel. Veterans of Foreign Wars Post 475 and American Legion Post 10 of Newark are named after Lieutenant James Allison O'Daniel.

LIEUTENANT JOSEPH M. FOX, BALLOONIST

Not all aviators piloted aircraft. The U.S. Army also had airborne balloonists. These were tethered balloons that rose to as much as four thousand feet to observe the enemy and to spot for artillery. Lieutenant Joseph M. Fox of Smyrna, Delaware, was a balloonist with the Fifth Balloon Company. Each company was equipped with one balloon. Five companies composed a squadron, and three squadrons made up a wing. In the field, balloon companies were allotted to the ground units they supported as needed. Only thirty-five companies made it to France with the American Expeditionary

Force. Of these, seventeen companies served at the front, making 1,642 combat ascensions.

The Fifth Balloon Company was organized at Fort Omaha, Nebraska, on November 4, 1917, with an authorized strength of six officers and ninety men.

About the first of January 1918, the company was equipped and trained for the field. After receiving a rousing sendoff from the people of Omaha, the unit departed on a special train for Garden City. After remaining there for ten days, they entrained in the wee hours of the morning for Hoboken, where the RMS *Adriatic* was boarded for a voyage to Liverpool. The squadron immediately went by daylight across England to Romsey.

On February 19, the company traveled by rail to Southampton and embarked on HMS *Hunslet*. As the ship crossed the English Channel that night, it narrowly missed another ship and docked at La Havre. The next day, the squadron proceeded by special train to a replacement camp at St. Maixent. After two weeks at this camp, the headquarters company of the squadron was split up so each company of the line had one hundred enlisted men. These companies then went to different stations, never to be reunited. Company A went to Camp Coetquidan to train with the artillery in the regulation of artillery fire.

At Coetquidan, the company received its transportation and the remainder of its equipment. This equipment was French. For almost five months, the balloon ascended every day, weather permitting, to assist the artillery in its regulation of fire or to carry out observation exercises with the aid of a projector.

On April 6, First Lieutenant Joseph M. Fox was assigned to the company as an observer. While at Camp Coetquidan, the balloon was in the air 237 hours and made thirty-nine regulations of fire, in addition to reporting on the general effectiveness of fire when it was not regulated by the balloon.

On July 25, the company left Geur by special train and proceeded to Toul. Arriving at Toul, the company proceeded by its own transportation to its new position near Raulecourt, being assigned to work with the Eighty-second Division. Lieutenant Fox was assigned as the chartroom officer. The company woodchoppers were kept busy, and the position was carefully laid out with three balloon beds and excellent retreat and advance itineraries. Forty kilometers of telephone wire were laid and kept in working order, giving all telephone liaisons that could be desired. In this position, the company had 128 hours in the air, made five reglages (adjustments) and spotted three enemy batteries in action.

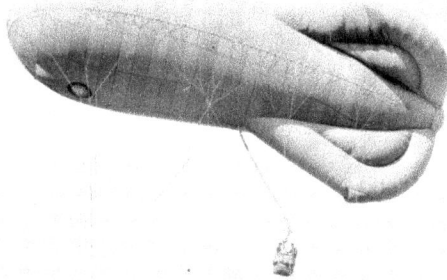

A tethered type R observation balloon. *Courtesy Library of Congress.*

On August 23, the company moved to a new position near Gironville, opposite to the point of the St. Mihiel Salient, and was assigned to work with the Fourth French Army. This position had never been occupied by a balloon company and was considered a very important but dangerous one. A camp was built, and telephone liaisons were established. On August 25, the balloon was shelled by a medium-caliber, long-range gun but was not damaged. The balloon was in the air for sixty-one hours, made one reglage and spotted one enemy battery in action.

On September 8, the company was transferred to the First Army Corps, First American Army, with Lieutenant McFarland commanding the corps balloons. The company was ordered to the vicinity of Dieulouard, near Pont-a-Mousson, where a position was to be established but no ascensions were to be made until the day of the attack.

During this time, on September 12, 1918, the famous aviator Frank Luke, later known as the "Balloon Buster," scored his first enemy balloon victory. Luke would become the second-leading American ace of the war, with eighteen victories. His first victory was witnessed and confirmed by Lieutenant Fox.

On the third day of the attack, September 14, the balloon was attacked and burned while adjusting fire at a distance of twenty-six kilometers on a railroad bridge directly west of Metz. First Lieutenants Maurice R. Smith and Joseph M. Fox, jumped and landed safely. On September 18, the balloon was shelled while in bed. The loss of gas in the balloon was the only damage done. On September 20, First Lieutenant Fox was relieved from duty with the company.

The Fifth Balloon Company had been in the AEF for over nine months, and during that time, the balloon had been in the air 506 hours and 11 minutes, had conducted fifty-seven regulations of fire and had spotted fifty-one hostile batteries in action. During this action, the company had not had a casualty among its officers or enlisted personnel, although the balloon had been burned four times, attacked unsuccessfully eight times and shelled once while in the air and the camp and balloon bed had been shelled five times.

At least one other Delaware native served as a balloonist. Thomas F. Naylor of Wilmington, Delaware, served in an army observation balloon squadron in France during the St. Mihiel and Argonne offensives. Naylor became a career military man, enlisting in the U.S. Navy in 1928 and serving through World War II aboard a submarine in the Caribbean, Iceland, Europe and the Pacific.

LIEUTENANT JOHN KNOX "MAC" MACARTHUR

John Knox MacArthur was born on January 14, 1891, in Columbia, Pennsylvania. He was educated at Yale College as an electrical engineer. John worked in Wilmington, Delaware, for a powder company. He entered service there on August 11, 1917. MacArthur was trained by officers of the Royal Flying Corps at Fort Worth, Texas. Lieutenant MacArthur was assigned to the Twenty-seventh Aero Squadron. MacArthur was sent overseas in February 1918. After additional training in England, the squadron arrived in France in the spring of 1918 and became a part of the First Pursuit Group on June 1, 1918. The following day, the squadron lost its first pilot and scored its first victory when it entered combat on the western front.

The First Pursuit Group was composed of four squadrons. The 27th Aero Squadron became known as the "Eagle Squadron," home of the second-highest scoring American ace of the war, Frank Luke The squadron joined the famous 94th Aero Squadron, led by Eddie Rickenbacker, the leading American air ace with twenty-six confirmed victories; the 95th "Kicking Mule"; and 147th "Terrier" Aero Squadrons in the First Pursuit Group.

MacArthur was awarded the Distinguished Service Cross:

> *For extraordinary heroism in action near Luneville, France, June 13, 1918. Outnumbered and handicapped by his presence far behind the German lines, Second Lieutenant MacArthur and three flying companions fought brilliantly a large group of enemy planes, bringing down or putting to flight all in the attacking party, while performing an important mission.*

In July 1918, most American pursuit squadrons—the Twenty-seventh included—were equipped with the Nieuport 28. A radical design departure from its forebear, the Nieuport 27, the N-28 was a light, nimble scout with a 160-horsepower Gnome Monosoupape 9N rotary engine. American pilots, not knowing any better, loved it. The French, on the other hand, had a newer model and refused to even take delivery of the N-28, sloughing them off on an American Air Service desperate for combat aircraft.

On July 17, 1918, MacArthur scored his fifth victory and became the Twenty-seventh Aero Squadron's first ace, flying the Nieuport 28. In a July 21, 1918, dispatch describing his fifth aerial victory, the squadron commander wrote:

> *The German Rumpler biplane was pursued by Lt. MacArthur below cloud level at about 4500 meters. The two machines exchanged fire when the Rumpler went over in a loop followed by MacArthur, firing as he flew within thirty yards of the enemy. He saw tracer bullets enter the enemy plane and it started to catch fire. He had fired 220 rounds to bring the Hun down.*

In a letter written on July 31, 1918, Captain Eddie Rickenbacker—of the group's sister squadron, the Ninety-fourth "Hat in the Ring" Aero Squadron—described MacArthur's last mission:

> *MacArthur had destroyed five enemy planes. He was admired immensely by all who knew him; the pilots who had flown over the lines with him looked upon him almost with reverence. He was cautious, quick, a clever pilot; also a dead shot. His example had made a wonderful organization out of the new pilots.*
>
> *Early in the morning of July 31, 1918, MacArthur led out his crack formation of six planes to try a strafing expedition upon the Aerodrome and Hangers of the Richthofen Circus which had just moved back from Coiny,*

occupying the Aeodrome north of Fismes. The Richtohofen Aerodrome was twenty miles within the German lines and the 27th Squadron Aerodrome, known as the "Fighting of Flying Circus" was 30 miles this side of German lines.

In a letter from one of them, telling what occurred, he stated that they had reached their objective without mishap and had strafed the hangers and billets of the Richthofen crowd until their ammunition was gone. Starting homeward they found a forty mile wind against them, being out over an hour, they could hardly hope to reach the home field against this gale before their fuel exhausted. Anticipating on reaching a nearer Aerodrome on their side of the line, they set their minds to this object; halfway to the lines they encountered several formations of enemy aircraft who were fully aware of their predicament and waited for them to come out. MacArthur led his formation up and down, back and forth, seeking for a place to break through, regardless of the tremendous odds. MacArthur led the attack, to enable his comrades to pass, but he and one comrade were killed in the air. The other pilots passed the enemy but their fuel exhausted and they fell inside German lines; one landing safely. This squadron formed the first pursuit group.

Newspaper reports in 1919 claim MacArthur died from his crash injuries in a German prison camp. His tombstone in Wilmington's Brandywine cemetery marks his death on August 9, 1918, a little more than a week after the crash. MacArthur was also awarded the French Croix de Guerre and was made a chevalier of the French Legion of Honor for his service.

FIRST LIEUTENANT LAURENCE ROBERTS

Laurence Roberts was one of those young men with a bright future. He planned to be an electrician. Roberts stood some five feet, ten and a half inches tall, with brown hair, blue eyes and a fair complexion. Born on December 27, 1895, he was the son of Mr. and Mrs. W.F.G. Roberts of Wilmington, Delaware. Roberts enlisted in the First Delaware Regiment, Delaware National Guard, in April 1914.

When the guard was mobilized for the Punitive Expedition to Mexico, Laurence was among the Delaware boys who went to the Mexican border in 1916. He had advanced to the grade of sergeant by this time. Arriving home, he entered officers training camp at Fort Meyer, Virginia, in field artillery. After six weeks, he applied for aviation and was subsequently sent to Toronto University, where he trained as a cadet in the British Royal Flying Corps. The United States had not yet entered the war.

Upon graduation, Roberts was sent to Fort Worth, Texas, and was commissioned as a first lieutenant on his twenty-second birthday. On January 31, 1918, he sailed for England as a member of the Twenty-second Aero Squadron. Once organized, the Twenty-second was sent to Toronto, Canada, on August 9 to begin formal training under the auspices of the Royal Flying Corps. In Canada, the squadron trained on the Curtis JN-4 and attended schools around the Toronto area. The men received instruction on engine and aircraft maintenance.

On October 19, the squadron finished its initial training and was sent to Hicks Field, near Fort Worth, Texas. Orders were received for overseas movement to France, and the squadron left for the Aviation Concentration Center, Long Island, on January 21, 1918. The squadron boarded the RMS *Adriatic* in New York Harbor, arriving in Liverpool, England, on February 16 and proceeding to camp, where the pilots were sent to advanced training schools in England, while the enlisted support personnel were sent to France for training with Royal Flying Corps units on the continent.

After more training in flying and aerial gunnery in Scotland, Roberts was ordered to the Seventeenth Aero Squadron in France on June 23.

As a day pursuit squadron, its mission was to engage and clear enemy aircraft from the skies and provide escort to reconnaissance and bombardment squadrons over enemy territory. It also attacked enemy observation balloons and performed close air support and tactical bombing attacks of enemy forces along the front lines.

The unit achieved a number of firsts. It was the first United States air squadron sent to Canada to be trained by the British, the first squadron to be completely trained prior to being sent overseas with its complete quota of trained pilots, the first squadron to be attached to British squadrons and the first to be sent into combat.

Roberts made his first trip over the lines on July 6. After several weeks of familiarization flights, the Seventeenth Aero Squadron entered combat on July 15, 1918, for the first time. The front was very quiet. Lieutenant Wilson brought down its first enemy airplane not far from Ostend, Belgium, about 9:45 a.m. on July 20 when the squadron encountered a formation of five German Fokker biplanes at approximately twenty-one thousand feet. That same day, the squadron suffered its first casualty of the war when Lieutenant

Glenn was seen diving deeply south of Ostend after being attacked by a German Fokker.

Lieutenant Laurence Roberts wrote on the death of a comrade killed in an accident in England, saying, "I hope that if I have to bump off, it will be at the front, where I can give a good account of myself." He didn't have long to wait.

On August 18, the Seventeenth was ordered to move to Auxi le Château Airdrome. The word came at 8:00 p.m., and the squadron pulled out at dawn. It arrived the next day and was settled in enough to send the first combat patrol over the lines on August 21, shooting down four enemy aircraft. Each pilot went on two patrols each day from dawn until disk. Over the next few days, the squadron shot down one enemy gas balloon each day, with the exception of the twenty-third, when it was put on low bombing dive and strafing missions all day. When flying the low-level attacks, the Seventeenth relied on other squadrons patrolling higher up to look out for the enemy's Fokkers while the squadron received ground fire from the enemy below.

August 26 was the squadron's most tragic day. Lieutenant Roberts had just returned from the hospital. It had rained during the night, and a gusty wind had begun to blow at dawn and was getting stronger. Low clouds, with gaps of blue between them, streamed thickly up from the southwest over the rolling hills beyond the aerodrome. The Besseneaux hangars bulged up and flapped; the tents were all swollen on one side and caved in against the wind. The airplane fabric that covered the so-called windows in the squadron office shack were bellied and tense; the little forest was full of the noise of the wind. It was blowing in fits at seventy or eighty miles an hour.

A History of the 17th Aero Squadron, 1918 records:

> *"Tip" got the patrol away in good style and they disappeared "eleven of them" over the trees. One machine returned before long with engine trouble, then another with guns jammed. Two hours passed. Then Goodie and Snoke arrived. Some of us will never forget the look in Goodie's light blue eyes, as he stood in the dusk, with his back against the door between the Squadron Office and the Pilots' Room. There was a huge map of the Third British Army front on the wall behind him. He pointed out where "it" happened, and slowly, bit by bit, from him and Snoke we got the story while he continued to stare, seeing us only a little, at the fight that was stamped almost visible on his eyes. He and "Snokie" seemed horrified and crest-fallen "all broken up" to be standing there, though each of them had put up a wonderful show, when Tip and Todd and Frost and Jackson and*

Bittinger and Roberts had not returned. Dixon too was missing; but after a long wait, in which we gave him up as lost, he came "hedge-hopping'" over the trees, having been driven down almost to the ground and having lost his way in the driving mist and high wind.

What really happened was this. Their mission, as we have said, was to cover low bombing operations. The squadron was called for a patrol about 16:30 with a mission to attack a lot of enemy on the lines and some friendly "low-strafers" in trouble on the Bapaume-Cambrai road. The squadron took off and upon reaching the lines, and shot down an enemy balloon. On crossing the line, five Fokkers were seen attacking friendly forces on the line. Immediately afterwards, a Camel was seen being attacked by the five Fokkers at a height of about 1,000 feet. This airplane was piloted by a friend of Lt. Roberts. The patrol at once went to the assistance of the Camel and attacked the enemy aircraft. Soon the Americans saw that the attack had been an ambush, for out of the clouds came about thirty more German airplanes. Several other flights of Fokkers were then seen diving from the clouds. A general engagement took place in which still other flights of Fokkers came down from higher altitudes. Three 17th pilots were shot down and a fourth only just succeed in getting back to the Auxi Airdrome with a number of Fokkers on his tail and firing continuously. All of the downed pilots were given up for lost, but about a month later three of the downed pilots were prisoners of war, but one was killed according to the "History of the American Expeditionary Forces Air Service." There are conflicting accounts of the action, with the Germans claiming as many as eight Sopwiths down and others saying six.

The fighting was terrific as the wind was blowing at fifty knots toward the German border while they maneuvered in the aerial dogfight. Roberts was among those lost, falling near the town of Cambrai. This was the last seen of him. By October 9th there was a report that he was a prisoner, but it was not known which camp.

Later information came to Robert's mother from an American who had searched German aviation files and reported:

On the day that your son was lost they reported having shot down eight Sopwith Camels, seven of which were in the region northeast of Bapaume. One was at Bapaume and the others at Lanicourt, Morchies, Beugny, Vauix, and Sapignies.

These towns lie some ten to fifteen miles northwest of Cambrai. The American correspondent went on to say:

> *2nd Lt. Harry Jackson, 2nd Lt. Howard Bittenger, and your son 1st Lt. Laurence Roberts, who was last seen over Cambrai, were all shot down in the same combat. (They are all listed on the casualty rolls of the 17th Aero Squadron as reported killed on August 26.) Lt. Knotts of the same squadron who had been taken prisoner soon afterwards and with whom I talked after his return, told me that he had learned from Lt. Schroeder, the German Intelligence Officer, who had questioned him, that all these three officers had been killed.*

On July 30, 1919, the U.S. War Department reported that First Lieutenant Roberts, Seventeenth Aero Squadron—missing since August 26, 1918—was presumed killed. German records did not confirm his death or place of burial.

Roberts's family was at a loss. They had lost a son and now could not even properly lament him because there was no known grave. There was only the faintest glimmer that he might remain alive. They would hope and pray.

In the meantime, the Laurence Roberts Post, American Legion Post 21, was founded in July 1920. In selecting an honoree, the name of Lieutenant Laurence Roberts was chosen because of his dauntless war record and because he had been a good friend and classmate to many of the members.

In the eighteen months since hearing from the War Department, many of the American troops returned home. Then on January 18, 1921, the Roberts family received a letter from George Larsen, formerly of the Second Canadian Mounted Rifles. Larsen stated that he had been

> *one of a detail of four sent out to pick up wounded and bury the dead in a certain territory. We came across the body of Lt. Roberts which was lying a short distance from a destroyed plane. He was identified by the identification tags…Lt. Roberts had been shot, probably by machine gun fire.*

The Robertses later received a letter from one of their son's fellow officers who wrote them that:

> *Bobbie (as he was called by his companions) was one of the most popular boys of the squadron, and a great favorite with all…He was secretly very proud of his mother and sister…I held him always in the highest*

esteem…He was a man in whom you can have the greatest pride—a
typical American…he put up a wonderful scrap and fought to the end as
a valiant son of the Western Democracy should.

It was not until the beginning of 1922 that his mother learned that Laurence was buried in the cemetery at Cambrai. Later, his remains, along with others, were moved to the American Cemetery near the little village of Bony, halfway between Cambrai and St. Quentin.

As was characteristic of many families in those days with the loss of a loved one in the battlefield, death hung around the home fires as well. The Spanish flu pandemic devastated populations in late 1918. The Roberts family was no exception. Roberts's sister was taken away by diphtheria, and three weeks later, his father was lost as well.

Roberts's mother visited her son's grave for the first time in 1927, courtesy of the American Legion. She last visited it as a member of the Gold Star Mothers in 1931 before her death in 1942.

Roberts's grave is marked beautifully in the little country cemetery near Bony. There, it is quiet and peaceful as the markers stand like silent sentinels all in neat rows as the breeze blows gently over them and Old Glory. Lieutenant Roberts's grave and thousands like it symbolize, according to President Lincoln, "the last full measure of devotion" to their country.

We were children, we ranged
Half in cloud, half in sun;
But now I am changed,
And must be gone.
—Robert Hillyer

7

IN THE LEE

HOMEFRONT

Governor John G. Townsend Jr. took office on January 16, 1917, and was destined to be Delaware's wartime governor, serving until 1921. His Republican administration was one of progressiveness and reform. All the major causes of the nineteenth century came to maturity during his tenure. Women's suffrage, Prohibition and better schools and highways were among the issues with which he grappled. He established Delaware's first highway administration and instituted a state budget system and an income tax. He reformed the state school system, which then had more administrators than teachers in 424 districts around the state. It was a top-to-bottom reorganization that created 180-day school years, built new facilities and hired more teachers, but it came at a high cost, both politically and economically. Townsend was a progressive who took unpopular positions on many of these reforms.

On the homefront, the Great War affected everyone in ways great and small. The most personal impact to families was the conscription or voluntary service of some ten thousand Delawareans. This created a strain on the job market as skilled employees went off to war. But it also created an opportunity for women and minorities to fill in the gaps. For the first time, women took what had traditionally been men's jobs. Many worked on the assembly lines of factories, producing trucks and munitions. Department stores employed African American women as elevator operators and cafeteria waitresses.

"Help him win by Saving and Serving—Buy War Savings Stamps," 1918. *Courtesy Library of Congress.*

The American Federation of Labor and nearly all labor unions were strong supporters of the war effort. They minimized strikes as wages soared and full employment was reached. Unions encouraged their young men to enlist in the military and opposed efforts to reduce recruiting or slow war production.

The economy surged into a boom cycle that brought jobs and opportunity. It also brought inflation at an average rate of 17 percent per year during the conflict, effectively doubling prices over its course.

The war also brought hardship and shortages despite the overall prosperity. The army required food and clothing, guns and ammunition, places to train and means of transport. The navy was expanded to protect American shipping and troop transports. The result was a rapid increase in federal spending, from $477 million in 1916 to a peak of $8,450 million in 1918. A combination of increased taxes, borrowing and the effects of an increased money supply (inflation) fueled this spending. The treasury created the famous Liberty Bonds. The first issue was a thirty-year bond bearing a 3.5 percent coupon, callable after fifteen years. There were three subsequent issues of Liberty bonds and one of shorter-term Victory bonds after the armistice. In all, the sale of these bonds raised over $20 billion for the war effort. Delaware was the only state to subscribe more than its quota of bonds.

Food, fuel, railroads and industry all came under tighter regulation as the government struggled to provide for the war effort and to mitigate shortages, manage natural resources, prevent logjams and redirect the economy toward war aims.

The Food Administration helped housewives prepare nutritious meals with less waste. Rationing was enforced, and victory gardens were encouraged. Under Herbert Hoover, the Food Administration encouraged "meatless, wheatless and sweetless" days. Nevertheless, the morale of the women remained high as millions volunteered for the Red Cross to help soldiers and their families. On the day war was declared, the Wilmington Red Cross offered classes at the YWCA on rolling bandages and preparing surgical dressings. There were so many volunteers that additional classes in other locations had to be scheduled. Delaware gave over $2 million in donations to the National Red Cross to buy medicine and supplies for the soldiers.

In Delaware, the war spurred a migration of people from rural to urban areas as they searched for new jobs and opportunities. Walter Deputy, whose memories of rural Delaware opened this book, recorded:

World War One changed the whole way of life for everyone. Grandpop's boys all left home to get married or to work in the war effort. They gave up farming and moved to Milford. Grandpop worked in construction, building Fort Saulsbury, near Slaughter Beach. The Deputy family moved to Wilmington prior to the declaration of war in 1917. Pop worked in the Powder Mills and Shipyards.

Not everyone left the farm. In an amusing incident, a rural Sussex County farmer was arrested for dodging the draft.

"HAD NOT HEARD OF THE WAR"

A young man in Delaware 24 years of age arrested in September 1918 for evading the draft, was released after he proved he did not know the United States was at war, and that he had not seen a newspaper in more than three years. His home was on a small island farm in the middle of a swamp near Newfound Delaware [also known as "Big Newfound Neck" west of Selbyville]. *He had not even gone to the village store for over three years, sending others after the few necessities of life required by him.*

He did not know there was a country named France, but said "he was willing to fight for America if he did not have to leave the United States." He was allowed to return to his home to straighten up any affairs needing attention and was ordered to report to Georgetown Delaware for military duty within a week.

From *Stories of the Great War for Public Speakers* by William Herbert Brown

SPIES, SABOTAGE AND PIRATES

The war fed fear and paranoia at home. Newspapers reported events from overseas, as well as reports of sabotage and espionage at home. The war was an incubator for rumor and fancy. A hermit living in a shack near Big Stone Beach was arrested as a spy after maps and soundings of Delaware Bay were found in his possession. During February 1916, hundreds were convinced they had spotted strange planes and zeppelins in the Delmarva skies. These phenomena proved to be the planets Venus and Jupiter in conjunction.

The *Philadelphia Inquirer* reported in June 1918:

> *Three small boys who had been reading Wild West novels and who had armed themselves with their dads' revolvers caused half the force of the Naval Station in Lewes to be called out, and aroused the whole countryside in a search of German spies around Nassau. After being spotted, the boys ran, and one of the soldiers shot at them and the kids shot back. Then they cleverly hid themselves in a nearby swamp and were not found. Eventually they gave themselves up and cried out their stories to their parents.*
>
> *All three had formed into a youthful band of highwaymen and started their career by putting log ties across the train tracks at Nassau to wreck the Philadelphia train to Lewes. As a train load of war materials was being shipped to the base at Lewes, the finding of the ties on the track gave belief at once to a theory that German spies had done the work.*
>
> *The boys will be taken before Magistrate Stewart at Georgetown tomorrow and will probably be paroled to their parents during good behavior.*

The *Philadelphia Inquirer* reported again in November 1918:

> *The war has made itself felt at Bethany Beach too. For a few brief weeks last summer the inhabitants lived in a state of continual excitement as strangely camouflaged ships were seen passing, and hydroplanes circled mysteriously over the beach. One day, cannonading was heard out to sea. The sheriff ordered all lights out that night as a raid or something else terrible was fully expected. But, the sun rose on the same peaceful homes the same undisturbed shore and sleepy small boys who were much disappointed.*

Sometimes the reports were based on fact.

THE GERMAN PIRATE IN DELAWARE WATERS

About one year before America entered the war, in March 1916, a German saboteur was afoot in the waters off the Delaware capes. Ernest Schiller was the lone German who captured the British freighter *Matoppo* for nineteen hours and came ashore near Lewes.

Originally, he and three other cohorts had laid a plot to take over another British liner, the ship known as *Pannonia*, and seize it by force from the officers and crew. There was thought to be £2,000 on board. They intended to spend the money to spread German propaganda. The brilliant nature of the scheme and seemingly high probability of its success were heartily reinforced by the fact that it was conceived under the influence of large amounts of alcohol poured in the saloons of Hoboken, New Jersey. On the big day, however, in the cold soberness of daylight, two of the conspirators got scared and a third dropped out.

Schiller had planned to sink the liner by holding up its officers and blowing it up or opening the seacocks. He remained determined despite the lack of support from his comrades.

Ernest Schiller's real name was Clarence Reginald Hodson. He was the son of an Englishman and a German mother, Emma Koch. He and his parents were residents of Petrograd, Russia, until age eleven. Schiller was smooth faced, well educated, tall and slender. He spoke excellent English as well as German. His parents separated, and he moved to Germany to live with his mother. He later became a naturalized British subject. He said, "I hate the English. I consider myself a German."

Schiller had some maritime experience, having studied marine engineering, and purportedly was a German spy in the United Kingdom, reporting shipping manufacturing to the fatherland. He fell under suspicion and came to the United States about nine months before his arrest.

Schiller said, "The British arrested me for singing 'Die Wacht am Rhein' in a London restaurant. They handled me. I made up my mind to get even. When I found myself on *Matoppo* I decided you can turn your misfortune into good fortune."

The German pirate Ernest Schiller, also known as Clarence R. Hodson. *Courtesy the author.*

In New York, he stole aboard the British freighter *Matoppo* bound for Vladivostok. After stowing away for four days in an upper deck lifeboat accompanied by some sandwiches and two revolvers, which the captain later described as "horse pistols," Schiller testified, "I thought I had four other men stowed away in other parts of the ship. I waited all day and into the night and at last I felt the sea rise and fall. I knew we were out and I went to work as soon as I was able to get my legs working."

Schiller added, "After I held up the captain in his cabin, the first officer came in and I covered him. 'Who in Hades are you?' he snapped. 'A German,' said I. He put his hands up and then I made them sing 'Die Wacht am Rhein.'" Schiller said the roundup was accomplished with relative ease as the captain and his chief officers were all "cowards." Indeed, the "pirate" mocked them all by pouring glasses of whiskey and suggesting that they all toast to one another's health and that of the Kaiser—at gunpoint.

He cowed the officers with his guns and smashed the wireless set. The captain believed Schiller had confederates on board with bombs. "The captain began to beg me not to kill any of them or to hurt his ship. He spoke of his wife and children and said if anything happened to his men, [the ship had a crew of about fifty] or his ship, he would lose his ticket and he and his wife and his children would be homeless."

Schiller continued:

> Going to the bridge, I asked the officer on duty if what the captain said was so, and he confirmed it, and I resolved that I would not kill anybody, but would probably land them and sink the boat. I planned to go ashore myself, taking two officers as hostages. And I had the ships course changed to the southwest.
>
> As the night went on I walked about and tried to think what I should do. The thought came to me of taking the ship to Mexico and selling her, but I learned that British Cruisers wait along the coast. At last I concluded it would be best for me to abandon ship. Changing the course to due west, I ordered the officers to go to sleep. Then I tried to sleep myself, with one eye open but I could not. As it grew light outside I heard the noise of the ships whistles and saw a vessel that I thought must be a British Cruiser. I resolved to ram her. But when she got nearer you could see she was a United States fruit boat.
>
> The morning was misty. I ordered full speed ahead for the coast, and the Chinese cook to make coffee for all hands. The Chinaman giggled as he stood over the galley fire. He was the only person aboard who appeared able to derive any fun out of the situation.

The officers appeared to be in a trance. I ordered the captain's gig lowered and the ship steered to a point near the lighthouse that was visible on the Delaware coast. But the captain said there were sandbars there. So he put me off in the small boat further up the coast. Then he played me false by breaking his word to me and hoisting a signal that there was a pirate aboard. The boat from the coast guard station put out and the men made me a prisoner.

After his nineteen-hour piracy, he added, "That meek and terrified English captain had broken his word! I had thought when an Englishman gave his word he would always keep it. I hate the English!"

Schiller denied that he was a pirate. "A pirate is a kind of bandit who would not stop at murder. The main reason why my plan to sink the *Matoppo* failed was because I did not want to kill anybody."

He was arrested at Lewes and then moved to New York and finally brought to Wilmington for trial in U.S. District Court, where he pleaded guilty. "Technically, I am a British subject. Therefore they would accuse me of treason and shoot me if was freed on this charge." Schiller received a life sentence. He attempted to escape from prison on July 10, 1916. He was working in the tailor shop of the Atlanta penitentiary when he decided to make his dash for freedom. It was reported that he made it past several guards and evaded considerable gunfire before successfully scaling a wall. But the impressive effort resulted in eventual capture. Schiller later told the warden that he had read about the arrival of the *Deutschland* and that he wanted to join its "gallant crew." He added that he was "determined" to escape and "seek vengeance" on those whom he hated: the English.

Calvin Coolidge commuted his life term in 1926.

Delaware Aeronautical Company Bombing Raid

Harry Atwood of the Delaware Aeronautical Company, a Claymont base flying school announced that the school would fly a mock air attack on Wilmington by dropping leaflets over the city. The Wilmington paper reported on June 26, 1917:

Thousands of Wilmingtonians witnessed a real demonstration of "bombing" a city as practiced on war-stricken towns of Europe when Harry Atwood, today, in charge of the aviation camp at Claymont and Thomas A. Birt, a former member of the Royal Flying Corps soared over this city and dropped "bombs" in the form of handbills. The demonstration by these daring airmen was made in the interest of the drive for recruits by the Delaware National Guard and the "bombs" were eagerly sought by everyone.

The handbills read as follows:

This handbill was dropped from an aeroplane over your head. It is not a German bomb, but it might have been. This is an appeal to the men of Wilmington between the ages of 18 and 45 to enlist in the Delaware Regiment before a bomb strikes us. Apply at the State armory, Twelfth and Orange Street, or at recruiting stations Old City Hall, or at 207 Maryland Avenue.

Today's flight was arranged by the officers of the National Guard in conjunction with Mr. Atwood to demonstrate to the citizens how easy it is for a city to be attacked from the air and to show that by rapid recruiting, this country could expect a victorious ending of the war with Germany.

Announcement of the sham air raid had caused everyone to be on the lookout for the airplane, and shortly before nine o'clock, a cry of "Here she comes!" was heard on all sides. Far to the northeast of the city, high in the heavens could be seen a small speck, and as it drew nearer and nearer, the planes of the air monster became visible. Soon the aviators were directly over the DuPont Building, and the *chug-chug* of the motors could be heard distinctly.

All business in the office buildings in the heart of the city ceased for a time. Trolley cars came to a stop, and housewives flocked to the streets to see the machine and secure the handbills that the aviators dropped over the city.

The machine made two complete circles over the city, turning each time over Front Street. As the last turn was made and the airman started to ascend on their return journey, one of the aviators waved his hand over the side of the machine to the populace below.

Besides the excitement of bombings and saboteurs, Delaware slogged on. The winter of 1917–18 was among the coldest on record. After twenty-nine continuous days of sub-freezing weather, the Delaware estuary was frozen with ice to the capes that even extended out to sea. Sussex County dealt with two feet of snow on the ground. The stranded pilot vessels were unable to guide ships through the estuary up to Philadelphia, temporarily halting shipping in the channel. The efforts made to get pilots out to waiting vessels nearly resulted in loss of life when huge floating cakes of ice carried the men out to sea, and it was only by turning around and fighting their way back that the men escaped with their lives.

War Comes to Liberty Street

By Marietta L. Olson, Wilmington, Delaware

Marietta Olson of Wilmington, Delaware, described life as an eight-year-old girl in a small town when the war arrived. She described her growing awareness of the war and the impact it had on her family and her Pennsylvania hometown. Her brief memoir illuminates life at home at that time.

Why was a youngster aware of war when there was no television showing war's horrors in our living room every night? With no radio constantly reporting war news, surely to many that period now seems to have been an age of innocence. Our parents conversations between themselves and with friends gave us what information we had plus a feeing of apprehension they shared. After war broke out in Europe we knew there was some evil force changing a world of which we had limited knowledge. Perhaps like "chicken little" we feared the sky might fall on us.

After the United States declared war on Germany, troop trains made long stops in Meadville. Trains refueled there and took on water in that age of steam engines. Every day these trains were emptied of troops for a period and the troops marched up our main streets, sometimes with bands, to let the men get some exercise after the long ride. Frequent parades of soldiers were the children's delight.

One day when my sister and I were baking cookies and cupcakes, we heard the clip-clip of marching feet going by a block a way from our house. On that pleasant day the march went beyond the business district into a residential area. We knew that those soldiers would have to return one block from our home. Our cookies and cupcakes were hurriedly put into a basket. Running to the corner, we presented them, as long as they lasted, to the smiling soldiers.

To our mothers, the soldiers represented a lot of hard work. The Red Cross met every troop train at the railroad station to serve coffee and doughnuts to the soldiers. The Red Cross was everyone's mother dressed in a white uniform. Sometimes we children were allowed to pass doughnuts to these khaki clad men who joked with us and told us of their families and hometowns. Most of us had traveled little and these far away homes were of interest to us. These same mothers who served at the station reported for hours of bandage rolling at the Red Cross Headquarters. Our outgrown clothes were washed and mended to be

The Red Cross Nurses Corps at the American Red Cross building at Delaware Avenue and Jackson Street, Wilmington. *Courtesy Delaware Historical Society.*

taken to the church. There the church women packed them to send abroad for the French, Belgian, and Armenian children.

The work of children on the Junior Red Cross was to report after school to "pick oakum." The dictionary says that oakum is "a jute or hemp fiber usually treated with tar or creosote." Our oakum was a straw like substance with tar mixed in, from which we picked out and discarded sharp or lumpy pieces. It was used medically for compresses which the ladies made. It was a messy job, but we felt patriotic and useful.

Women's knitting needles flew; hands were never idle. Girls too knitted the endless number of khaki wool sweaters, scarves and socks needed by the soldiers. Although mother obligingly let me try to knit a scarf in the spirit of service to some unknown doughboy, my effort was a total flop whose squiggly edges my aunt had to re-knit completely.

However, did not the poster opposite my bed display a grim Uncle Sam pointing his finger at me saying, "I need you to join the Army?" Since joining the army was impossible of me, any other efforts I could make were important. There was also a poster of a pretty girl in a sailor's cap urging the young to join the Navy. Other posters adorned the walls of my brothers' rooms and the rooms of all their friends.

We saved every penny to buy Thrift Stamps at school for 25 cents each. These stamps added up to other denominations which might eventually become a War Bond. Rallies were held with the biggest name attractions possible to exhort our parents to buy War Bonds.

My father, as a physician, had his war service cut out for him on the home front. Not only did the doctors at home care for their own patients but took on all patients of the younger doctors who had gone to war. In those days, if you were sick enough to go to bed, the doctor called on you at home to diagnose your trouble, whatever the distance he must travel. After the terrible influenza epidemic of the war years broke out, this was an even more Herculean task for these hometown doctors.

Two phones rang all day and all night in our dining room and in my parent's bedroom. No meal at our house was eaten undisturbed, no night's sleep uninterrupted. Once when my mother became ill, father diagnosed that illness as "telephonitis."

With influenza widespread, serving local people became an even more acute problem. It worsened with soldiers being removed from troop trains when they were simply too sick to go further. The hospitals overflowed and an emergency hospital was set up in the school gymnasium. In this large bare room endless rows of cots were set up and our mothers became nurses' aides.

I wonder why I was allowed in there, perhaps to carry a message to my mother or father. The picture of that bleak bare building filled with sick men so far from home and so miserable impressed on my memory. When I was one of the two in our family to get the disease, I felt sorrier for those sick soldiers without a mother to bring them tempting food and a good bed to snuggle in.

Rationing was a part of our wartime lives. In a small town with chicken, eggs, fresh vegetables and some home grown meats, we suffered from rationing much less than city people. Victory gardens were widely advised and praised. To us, who had always had two large gardens it meant just a larger one and more canning and drying. Additional sugar could be had for canning but sugar was at a premium. The greatest personal tragedy of the war as far as I was concerned was when my mother announced that there was simply no sugar for my birthday cake that year. Now to have a birthday four days before Christmas was bad enough—but to have no cake was unthinkable. My birthday parties were at a minimum on such an impossible date but the day had always been crowned with a cake at *our family celebration. Luckily a friend of my mother's came to the rescue, saying: "Oh, I have enough extra sugar for Marietta's cake." The day was saved and the lady became a saint in my book.*

I can still recite the poem, "In Flanders fields the poppies grow between the crosses row on row…" We became aware that war was sad when a soldier we saw marching might become a cross in a far away country. We studied European geography with a new interest. Sadness was balanced by the cheerfulness of war songs like "Over There" and "Tipperary" which we all sang.

Our two older brothers were almost enlistment age. The oldest one, a freshman in college begged my parents to enlist in an ambulance unit. My father finally gave his permission to this son who he felt was too young for such service. All of that rainy gloomy day my mother wept and we all sorrowed [sic] for something we did not fully understand. But fate intervened: my brother's prospective unit was filled one man before his application. Instead, he came back to college where he and my younger brother were in the Army after the United States' entrance into the war. They were in uniform under Army regulations in barracks that were former fraternity houses. However, the war ended before they saw active duty.

One terrible event of which we did have some understanding was the explosion of a large munitions plant. Many of the older boys, some close friends of my brothers, had gone to take summer jobs there. They urged my brothers to come with them since the pay was good. The explosion took the lives of all of these local young men. We did not see a factory blown up on a television screen, but we saw the stricken faces of these boys' parents, and we had nightmarish pictures in our minds of these young people we knew being blown to bits. War was no longer glamorous to us; it was trouble, danger and sadness.

This tragic loss of friends came closer to us than the reported German atrocities in Belgium and France. We pictured the Huns as cruel and heartless monsters doing terrible things to innocent people. But those innocent people were people we read about. We did not know them.

Names of people and places hitherto unknown to us became part of family conversation. Pershing was a hero. Adults talked about Petain, Clemenceau, Foch, Haig, Lloyd-George and others. Maps of France hung on the walls of almost every home. The Allied armies were indicated in colored thumb tacks, the Germans and their allies by others. As the victories and losses at the Somme, Château-Thierry, Belleau Woods and the Argonne were reported in American papers, the thumb tacks were moved to give us a visual idea of what was happening "over there."

Politics became more interesting. Should Wilson have kept us out of the war so long? Were his policies in war the right ones? In the political campaign of 1916 my neighbor across the street wore her Wilson button while our family displayed Hughes buttons on their coats. I can remember having almost a fist fight with the neighbor girls trying to snatch each others' presidential campaign buttons. I may have been cheered on by my Republican friends but my mother did not cheer about the hole torn in my coat. We lost the election and Wilson won.

This was the last war in which towns sent their own military units to the battlefield. Too many towns lost most of their young men if the engagement of that particular company was a very dangerous one. Company B of the National Guard went off to war with great local fanfare. We all gathered in the park in the center of town to say farewell to these men, and to give them our blessing. They were, "our soldiers" who later became involved in the fighting in the Argonne sector in France and suffered many casualties.

The discouraging days of a terrible war made months longer. People were tired and prayed for an ending to the fight against the stubborn enemy. Mother worried about father's exhaustion in providing endless medical services.

Finally the day came when schools were dismissed, church bells rang, factory whistles shrilled in the air. Jubilant townspeople roamed the streets, laughing crying, shouting. Armistice Day, November 11, 1918 was a day of celebration and excitement. Probably there were more emotions unleashed in public on that day than I have never seen since. The giant presence of War fell to the ground leaving in his footsteps destruction and sorrow. He was not to arise again in my childhood…but, alas, later.

One may have been fortunate to escape the immediate hazards of war, but few could avoid the impact of a global disease.

SPANISH INFLUENZA PANDEMIC

One factor that no one could control and that was a nearly universal malady was the Spanish flu, which killed tens of millions globally. One in four Americans contracted the disease. The result was a half million dead in the

Delaware in World War I

United States. The casualty figures for our soldiers were forty-four thousand flu victims versus fifty thousand combat victims.

The flu first presented itself in the spring of 1918. In Delaware, thousands of cases were reported, and it killed over 2,000 people. In October 1918 alone, 1,223 Delawareans died. On October 2, the *Wilmington Morning News* reported 3,500 cases in the city and 4,500 in the state. Public meetings were banned. On October 20, some seventy bodies were lying unburied due to a shortage of coffins and gravediggers. Delmar, with a population of 2,000, reported 800 cases. Regardless of the numbers, though, Delaware acted to contain the flu just as many other states had. On October 3, 1918, the Delaware State Board of Health met in an emergency session to stem the death toll from influenza. It shut down most of the state:

> *Whereas: A very serious epidemic of influenza is now raging in the state of Delaware…to protect the health of the entire citizenship of Delaware…all schools, all theatres, all churches, all motion picture houses, all dance halls, all carnivals, fairs and bazaars, all billiard rooms and pool rooms, all bowling alleys in the entire State of Delaware shall be closed and kept closed until further notice.*

This order remained in effect for more than three weeks. Yet even these careful precautions were not enough to control the disease. As the situation in Delaware worsened, Delaware became so overwhelmed that the health department tried to divert influenza patients to Philadelphia hospitals. The flu, however, knew no state lines. Philadelphia was unable to come to Delaware's rescue, as it too was completely overrun by the disease.

In particular, the flu seemed to target the young, strong and otherwise healthy. The army had constructed huge training camps, especially in the south, some housing as many as fifty thousand troops in close quarters in tents and barracks. City boys and country boys from all over the country comingling, with varying degrees of vulnerabilities, created an explosive mix for the disease. The main strain of the flu surfaced at Camp Funston in Kansas in March and rapidly spread to other camps. By the end of the month, twenty-four of thirty-six of the largest camps had outbreaks. Some 40 percent of American soldiers had landed in Brest by April 1918, bringing the disease to the Allied armies in the field as well as the German army.

Most of the victims from this first wave survived their bout, lending increased immunity to the more deadly second wave that arrived in September. Influenza reached Camp Upton, Long Island, New York, the

130

training camp for many Delaware recruits, in mid-September. This was precisely the beginning of the peak period of deadly infection, lasting until early December. The epidemic lasted until 1920, killing an estimated fifty million people worldwide. In Philadelphia, it raged through the navy yard. In one week in October, Philadelphia recorded 4,587 deaths from the disease.

In the American Expeditionary Force, four of every one thousand soldiers died of the flu. In only some ten weeks—between September 1 and November 11—nine thousand died in France and twenty-three thousand died in the United States from the disease. In some units, the rate of fatality was up to 32 percent. The following personal account helps illustrate how the citizens dealt with the epidemic.

A Time to Mourn and Time to Dance

By Louise S. Carrigan, Wilmington, Delaware

As a ten year-old at the time of the Great Influenza Epidemic of nineteen eighteen, I still retain vivid memories of many loved ones and acquaintances who were struck down so quickly. And as a country preacher's kid I had the opportunity of visiting the homes of stricken families with Dad.

I was particularly stunned and saddened whenever two afflicted family members were laid out to the silent rest side by side in the parlor. And I shall never forget one dear little baby girl who had succumbed to the disease when she was only a few weeks old, lying on an ironing board dressed in her christening dress, her small hands folded over a white flower.

During the epidemic all schools in our area were closed—but churches never. Special services were held for the deceased whenever possible. Sunday school and regular church services were conducted as usual.

However, children of the community still had their fun. We skated on the frozen ponds in winter. My mother had "taffy pulls" for my brothers and my young friends. (Her special taffy concoction was made of molasses, a little vinegar and a little home churned butter.) We also played "parlor games." Mother played the popular World War I tunes on the "pump organ." She also played an auto harp that her father gave her on her thirteenth birthday.

Brother Bill and I had our chores to do, like keeping the gray mare fed and groomed for trips to the country store or any other emergency. As I loved all animals it pained me whenever a rooster or a hen had to sacrifice its life for our sustenance. Sometimes Dad would provide a squirrel or a rabbit.

Christmas that year did not involve the usual gift giving and "goodies." Yet on Christmas morning it was nevertheless a treat to find two oranges each in our stockings—plus nuts and sticky animal candy. While we children were happily consuming the latter, Mother followed us around with a wet cloth in her hand, wiping everything that we touched. We had a cedar Christmas tree that year, donated by some friendly farmer and trimmed in gold and silver stars made by Mother's father when she was a girl. Mother and I also made toy dolls and animals from clothes, pine, cotton and bits of cloth.

Then came a frightful turn of events in our small family. Mother herself became a victim of the dreaded flu "bug." Doctors were working night and day. The hospital was overcrowded and it was miles away. When the doctor was finally contacted and he arrived at our door, Dad would not let him come in, for it required only one look to realize that the busy overworked doctor was intoxicated with his nearly continuous lack of sleep and his valiant attempt to ward off his patient "bug." One could hardly blame the poor man for his condition.

So dear Mother's fate was in the hands of God and her family. Dad had heard that cooked onion "poultices" could sometimes break up lung congestion. The pungent aroma soon penetrated our house day and night. We took turns keeping vigil at her bedside. Bill and I would attend to her by day, and when I would walk past her bedroom door at night, I could see Dad down on his knees, praying for her recovery. Thankfully, Mother managed to pull through and even lived to the ripe old age of ninety seven. The rest of us never contracted the disease but only a little weakness and slight dizzy spells.

One glorious day we heard church bells chime and whistles blow, letting the world know that World War I had ended…and our oldest brother who had served as a U.S. Army medical corpsman in England and France would soon be back safely with his family.

The influenza outbreak touched nearly every family, but other factors would have a more lasting effect.

Social trends with roots in the nineteenth century were accelerated by the war. New Castle County joined the two downstate counties in voting to prohibit alcoholic beverages, leaving only the city of Wilmington as a place to buy a drink. On March 9, 1918, Delaware became the ninth state

Women marching in national suffrage demonstration in Washington, D.C., on May 9, 1914. *Courtesy Library of Congress.*

to ratify the Prohibition amendment—the Eighteenth Amendment—to the U.S. Constitution, which became law on January 16, 1919.

Women were granted the vote by the Nineteenth Amendment, ratified on August 18, 1920. They went to the Delaware polls for the first time in November of that year.

The end of the decade brought to a culmination point many social trends, but it also brought an end to the biggest threat of all.

8

FAIR WINDS

The Great War, which had been a stalemate for four years, ended abruptly. It was less a decisive battlefield victory and more a capitulation of the exhausted. The conflict would echo for generations as it altered the social fabric of Delaware and the nation.

ARMISTICE

Marshal Ferdinand Foch sent the following message on November 12, 1918:

> *OFFICERS, NON-COMMISSIONED OFFICERS SOLDIERS OF THE ALLIED ARMIES*
> *After having resolutely stopped the enemy you have for months attacked him without respite, with an untiring faith and energy. You have won the greatest battle of history and saved the most sacred of causes: the liberty of the world. Be proud. You have covered your colors with immortal glory. Posterity will hold you in grateful remembrance.*
> *The Marshal of France. Commander-in-Chief of the Allied Armies.*
> *F. FOCH*

The armistice brought peace at last, but the Great War continued to have an impact on Delaware. The Fifty-ninth Infantry Pioneers soldiered on for nearly nine months in the occupation garrison in France and Germany. There was much work to do to tidy up the battlefields and salvage and clear munitions and equipment. In fact, the Pioneers took their worst casualties of the war in an accidental mine explosion on January 22, 1919. Wilmington soldiers Thomas Davis, Harvey Hadley, Howard Johnson, John Chandler and three other regiment soldiers from Company I were killed in a mine explosion in Rehon, near Toul, France.

The men of the Fifty-ninth finally returned home in July 1919 to a triumphant celebration where they were once again feted in Wilmington. The Washington Street Memorial Bridge, dedicated to Delaware's war dead, was opened in Wilmington and formally dedicated on Memorial Day 1922 as the Washington Memorial Bridge. A parade was held, and many returning veterans marched in the ranks as members of the Delaware National Guard.

An Armistice Day Letter from John "Iron Mike" O'Daniel at the Front

John Wilson O'Daniel was born in Newark, Delaware, on February 15, 1894. He attended Delaware College in Newark, Delaware, where he played varsity football and earned the nickname "Mike." He enlisted in the Delaware National Guard in 1913 with Company E, First Delaware Infantry. On July 19, 1916, he was mobilized and served as a corporal and sergeant with the First Infantry at the Mexico border in Deming, New Mexico. O'Daniel was honorably discharged from service on his twenty-third birthday, February 15, 1917.

After graduation from Delaware College in 1917, O'Daniel was commissioned a second lieutenant of the Infantry Reserve on August 15.

He shipped out for overseas duty and participated in the St. Mihiel and Meuse-Argonne offensives. He was wounded at St. Mihiel on September 12, 1918. His nickname, "Iron Mike," awarded by his peers, was said to be a result of his actions at St. Mihiel, where he fought for twelve hours, even though he was hit in the face by a German machine gun bullet and severely wounded. He was awarded the Distinguished Service Cross for his actions as well as the Purple Heart.

In a letter to Dr. Samuel Chiles Mitchell, the president of Delaware College, O'Daniel described Armistice Day in France and how he and his men experienced the last hours of the war.

Longwy, France
Nov. 26, 1918

My Dear Dr. Mitchell

Your two kind letters I rec'd. while on the line. They were great too as at that time every little bit did help some. I got the last one the day before we went over the top or rather the day we crossed the Meuse R. You will have to pardon me if I use a little slang now and then to express myself. I feel that I would like to tell you about our last little scrap. It lasted from Nov. 5 to 11 and consisted of chasing the Bosch for all we were worth. We had him bluffed and on the run when the bell rang. We had chased him and fought him for 20 kilometers in the 5 days, thru rain and cold.

Our boys never complained once, but kept right after him. My company had the honor of being the advanced guard on the crossing of our Regiment over the Meuse R. and also capturing Hill 260 which was a great point of vantage. The last time we went over the top was Nov. 10, at a town called Louppy. My company captured most of the town and in it a wonderful old chateau with paintings, high walls, and a wonderful terrace, motes [sic] immense gates and other things that go to make up a chateau. The boys went over that last time with a yell. Fritz went a flying and our men after him. When night came we found ourselves thru the town with the Bosch dug in on the far side of it. My company was dug in inside a little church yard with Fritz about 300 yards away.

Machine guns were popping and everything sitting pretty when night came on and then plenty of shells. Morning and 9:30 came, someone came to my P.C. and told those of us there that Armistice was on and things would be over soon. One of my Sgts. who has been awarded the Medal of Honor for bravery said in his characteristic slow drawl, "Wal, what it takes to make peace I've got buckled around me." He had it too. 100 rounds of U.S. Ammunition on the outside and about 150 lbs. of solid American all the way thru. That is the way we all felt about it when the end came.

Orders came to go after ammunition. Six men went for it. We knew what that meant—over the top again. Ten o'clock and a runner came puffing in with a message. It read—"Armistice Official Announced, Take affect at 11 a.m. Fire shot for shot" I read it aloud, no one said a word. We just looked at each other and then sent the word to the men around us. There wasn't a sound. At 11 a.m. we hear a noise out front and upon looking over the wall of the cemetery of the little church saw about 200 Bosch without arms walking around and laughing and talking. All was over.

It reads like a novel, but true it is. A coincidence is the dates on which the Armistice came—11th month, 11th day, 11th hour and 11th Infantry. All noise had ceased—the world was at peace, and here we are on our way to the Rhine.

It might interest you to know that I have been promoted to the rank of Capt. and have been fortunate enough to have been decorated with the Dist. Service Cross.

I have only the Lord to thank for it all. I can't realize it. But here we are. You may notice that I have mentioned my company. I do so because I am proud of that little bunch of men. Why shouldn't I be with one man with the Medal of Honor, 3 with D.S.C.'s and 12 with Citations. They all deserve it too. All Americans are the same. The most wonderful fighters and the best fellows on earth.

This is captured Bosch paper and it happens to be all I have at present, so excuse everything.

Thanking you again for your kind letters, best regards to the old Institution and all my friends.

Sincerely,
J. Wilson O'Daniel

O'Daniel returned to the United States with the Eleventh Infantry on September 1919. He would later lead the famous Third Division, "Rock of the Marne," in World War II and retire as a lieutenant general.

A Homefront Perspective

The following excerpted account was written by Charles A. Owens Jr. of Rehoboth Beach, Delaware, and offers the reaction of a schoolboy from Wilmington to the premature news of "peace at last."

I was a student in the sixth grade of the Friends School at Fourth and West Streets in Wilmington Delaware. Most of the students in our school were extremely emotional in their feelings concerning the fighting overseas. Many had close relatives or friends fighting the battles we read about or heard discussed amongst our elders. Many boys were collecting war posters and trading between themselves in order to have the greatest number of hard-to-find specimens. Nearly all students wore miniature American flags pinned on their clothing. Several of us sported a really prized brazen possession: a pin shaped like a dark silhouette of a spiked Prussian helmet with the words, "Hell mit der Kaiser" printed across its face. We seldom wore this particular item to school but displayed it as soon as we were outside and beyond the jurisdiction of the school authorities. Like all students our age, our minds were much more attuned to the progress of our armies than the then much less interesting lessons we were compelled to learn in school.

During this time, my father was a stockbroker and maintained his office in the DuPont building at 10th and Market Streets. He was in a partnership under the name, "Owens, Anderson and Rumford." The firm had a direct wire to New York City. In 1918 there was no television and radio itself was then mostly a novelty enjoyed by a few dedicated "buffs." Those who owned radios were primarily interested in contacting other "hams" and then bragging about reaching someone in Pittsburgh or far away Florida. Much news came over the direct wire to my father's firm. Such items were received long before the Wilmington newspapers were published in the late afternoon.

On Thursday, November 7, 1918 I was deeply involved with my classmates in some lesson when there was a knock on the classroom door. Our teacher opened the door a few inches, held a brief and indistinguishable conversation with the unseen intruder, and then returned to her desk. She rapped for silence and said, "Charles Owen, please come here!" Startled, I rose and approached her desk. Quietly, so other students could not hear, she informed me that I was to report at once to Mr. Herschel Norris, the principal of the school.

I was thunderstruck! A student was never called to the Principal's office unless he or she had committed some dreadful offense. Slowly I went to the door, quietly opened it and went down the hall towards Mr. Norris' office, conscious that the eyes of all my classmates had been riveted on me as I left the room. They all knew I must be heading toward a meeting with the "final authority" and each was wondering in his own mind what terrible crime was responsible for my summons to "the carpet."

Mr. Norris was, in my eyes, a rather large and forbidding person. Expecting a reprimand for an unknown breach of conduct, imagine my surprise when he said, "Charles, your father is on the telephone and wishes to speak to you." My next panic-stricken thought was: "Dear Lord, what had I done wrong at home?"

Thankfully, my father sounded extremely happy and soon allayed my fears of punishment. He informed me that the reason he had called was to let me know that wonderful news had just been received over his New York wire: The armistice had been signed and THE WAR WAS OVER! He wanted me to be the first one in school to hear the glorious news. He then instructed me to put Mr. Norris back on the phone. Evidently father convinced Mr. Norris to let me make the rounds of the classrooms and announce the great news. Accordingly, the principal and I went from room to room, and after what we had been admitted he would say, "Class, Charles has something to tell you." Imagine my pride in being the one to break the most important news in the whole world to my friends! Such shouting and cheering we had never been heard in those staid walls before. I was the hero of the hour; I was in seventh heaven.

School was dismissed and most of the joyous young headed for home shouting the glad tidings at the top of their lungs. Church bells were beginning to peal. Factory whistles were blowing. Locomotives in the Pennsylvania freight yards were adding to the noise with their whistles and bells. Anything that could make a noise was put to that use at once. Amid all this frenzy, I made my way to father's office, per instructions he had given me on the telephone. Once there, we hurried to his automobile and headed for home. Then we bundled my mother and sister into the car and headed back downtown.

By the time we reached the vicinity of 10th and Market, we were blocked by the crowds pushing towards a vantage point on Market Street itself. An impromptu parade had developed moving south on Market. Trucks and autos, alternately raced their motors and then cut them off. This made the engines backfire with a tremendous BANG! Trolley cars clanged their bells madly. Private autos kept up a continuous cacophony with their horns. "Snake-dancing" was going on everywhere. People shouted themselves hoarse. Utter hysteria prevailed. It was a wonder that people were not injured in the frenzied melee that was taking place. Later we learned that in New York City, Fifth Avenue too was jammed with the greatest crowd ever seen up to that time. The whole country was crazy with joy.

Late in the afternoon, the local newspapers began to appear on the streets. They refuted the news of the Armistice. People became angry and refused to believe the newspapers. Several unlucky newsboys had their papers torn to shreds by upset bystanders. Nothing could stop the celebration that continued to go on unabated. Although my parents had taken me and my sister home late in the afternoon, the frenzy lasted long into the night. On Friday, November 8, there was continued confusion concerning the Armistice. When I returned to school, I was still somewhat of a hero in the eyes of my fellow students and naturally basked happily in the warmth of their adoration.

However, on Saturday the 9th, the President of the United States issued a statement that the news of the signing of the surrender was false. I was heartbroken. How could I return to school and face my classmates? How could I possibly handle their taunts? I was never so miserable in my life. I prayed at night to the Lord that somehow He would come to my aid. He did!

On Monday, November 11, 1918, the official notice of the signing of the terms of the Armistice was announced throughout the land by big black headlines in all the newspapers. This time though, most of the citizens were too weary physically and too spent emotionally from the first Armistice celebration to arouse the same degree of enthusiasm for the second one. However, the happy turn of national events fortunately caused my teachers and fellow students to forget my part in spreading the news of the "false armistice" and I felt glad to be "off the hook."

Delaware Heroes of the Great War

In every war, we recognize valor and we honor the dead. Below are some selected samples of that valor followed by examples of Delaware's gratitude toward its servicemen.

Distinguished Service Cross and the Navy Cross

No Delawareans are on record to have received the Medal of Honor, but ten sons of Delaware were awarded the nation's next-highest honor for their actions during World War I. The Distinguished Service Cross is the second-highest military award that can be awarded to a member of the United States Army; it's awarded for extreme gallantry and risk of life in combat with an armed enemy force. Actions that merit the Distinguished

Service Cross must be of such a high degree that they are above those required for all other U.S. combat decorations but do not meet the criteria for the Medal of Honor. The Distinguished Service Cross was established by President Woodrow Wilson on January 2, 1918. General Pershing, commander in chief of the Expeditionary Forces in France, had recommended that recognition other than the Medal of Honor be authorized for the armed forces of the United States for valorous service rendered in like manner to that awarded by the European armies.

THOMAS D. AMORY was a second lieutenant in the Twenty-sixth Infantry Regiment, in Archie Roosevelt's Company, from Wilmington, Delaware. He was a graduate of the Virginia Military Institute. He was awarded the Distinguished Service Cross for extraordinary heroism in action near Verdun, France, on October 2, 1918. Lieutenant Amory took out a patrol of sixty-four men, penetrating enemy lines for the purposes of reconnoitering terrain over which an advance was to be made the following morning. When the patrol was fired on by machine guns from all sides, this officer led three of his men forward to clear the machine gun nests, placing the rest of his men under cover. He succeeded in overcoming one of these nests and killing the enemy, but as he was advancing on another gun, located in a house about ten yards away, he was killed by a machine gun bullet, his last words being, "We'll take that nest or die trying." Amory had been seriously wounded the previous May but had returned to action with his company. He is buried in the Meuse-Argonne American Cemetery and Memorial.

EDWIN H. COOPER was a captain in the Twenty-sixth Division, United States Army, of Wilmington, Delaware. He was awarded the Distinguished Service Cross for extraordinary heroism in action while serving with the photographic section, Signal Corps (Attached), Twenty-sixth Division, AEF, near Torcy, France, on July 18–20, 1918. On 18 July, Captain Cooper advanced fearlessly under enemy fire to an exposed position in a shell hole in front of the attacking troops in order to carry out a photographic mission. While in this position, he went to the rescue of a wounded man and carried him to the shelter of a shell hole about one hundred yards to the rear. Later, he assisted in the evacuation of enemy prisoners. On July 20, he again advanced to a forward position in order to secure pictures of the attacking troops. His gallant conduct stimulated the morale of the advancing troops.

George H. Fergusen was a second lieutenant in the Sixth Infantry. He lived on East Main Street in Newark, Delaware. He was awarded the Distinguished Service Cross for extraordinary heroism in action while serving with Sixth Infantry Regiment, Fifth Division, AEF, near Romagne, France, on October 14, 1918. After being painfully wounded in the leg early in the attack, Lieutenant Ferguson continued forward, leading his platoon through an unusually heavy artillery and machine-gun fire. Later, he left a shell hole in which he had taken refuge and administered first aid to soldiers who had fallen near him until forced to abandon his work because of exhaustion.

Leroy Jones was a private first class in Company E, 115th Infantry. He lived at 28 Kempmere Road, Wilmington, Delaware. He was awarded the Distinguished Service Cross for extraordinary heroism in action while serving with Company E, 115th Infantry Regiment, Twenty-ninth Division, AEF, near Verdun, France, on October 8, 1918. While his platoon was being held up by machine-gun fire, Private Jones voluntarily left his position, and crawling through intense machine-gun fire, he single-handedly captured two machine guns, killing four of the enemy and taking both crews.

John Knox MacArthur was a second lieutenant of the Twenty-seventh Aero Squadron, First Pursuit Group, U.S. Army. He was awarded the Distinguished Service Cross for extraordinary heroism in action near Luneville, France, on June 13, 1918. Outnumbered and handicapped by his presence far behind the German lines, Second Lieutenant MacArthur and three flying companions fought a large group of enemy planes, bringing down or putting to flight all in the attacking party, while performing an important mission. An aerial ace with six victories, MacArthur was also awarded the French Croix de Guerre and was made a chevalier of the French Legion of Honor for his service. He died from his wounds as a German prisoner and is buried in Brandywine Cemetery in Wilmington.

John W. O'Daniel was a second lieutenant with the Eleventh Infantry. He lived on East Main Street in Newark, Delaware. He was awarded the Distinguished Service Cross for extraordinary heroism in action while serving with the Eleventh Infantry Regiment, Fifth Division, AEF, near Bois-St. Claude in the St. Mihiel salient on September 12, 1918. After being severely wounded in the head early in the action, Lieutenant O'Daniel continued in command of his platoon, leading his men for several hours until forced to give in to complete physical exhaustion, thus displaying most exceptional courage, determination and devotion to duty. O'Daniel would later lead the Third Infantry Division in World War II and retire as a lieutenant general.

GEORGE OGDEN was a corporal with Company H, 110th Infantry Regiment, United States Army. He was from Wilmington, Delaware. He was awarded the Distinguished Service Cross for extraordinary heroism in action while serving with Company H, 110th Infantry Regiment, Twenty-eighth Division, AEF, near Montblainville, France, on September 27 and near Baslieux, France, November 2–9, 1918. While acting as battalion scout, Corporal Ogden succeeded in driving away the crews of two enemy machine-guns by sniping. Operating one of these guns himself and a sergeant the other, they materially assisted in repulsing an enemy counterattack. On another occasion, while leading a patrol of ten men on the Vesle River, Corporal Ogden succeeded in getting on the flank of the enemy and, by rifle fire, forced about one hundred to retreat from a trench in disorder, inflicting many casualties. Later, he succeeded in getting in the rear of the enemy positions, remaining in hiding until night and then returned with valuable information relative to the enemy's positions.

LEROY E. SIMMERS was a private with the 116th Ambulance Company, 104th Sanitary Train, of Wilmington, Delaware. He was awarded the Distinguished Service Cross for extraordinary heroism in action while serving with 116th Ambulance Company, 104th Sanitary Train, Twenty-ninth Division, AEF, near Haumont, France, on October 11, 1918. Private Simmers, a stretcher bearer, gave proof of great courage and unhesitating devotion to duty under heavy shell fire by assisting three wounded soldiers to a place of safety, he himself being wounded while so doing. After receiving first aid, he returned to the shell-swept area and continued in the work of rescuing the wounded.

JOHN H. TEMPLE was a private with Company I, 312th Infantry Regiment of Marshalton, Delaware. He was awarded the Distinguished Service Cross for extraordinary heroism in action while serving with Company I, 312th Infantry Regiment, Seventy-eighth Division, AEF, near Grand Pre, France, on October 23, 1918. After his platoon had reached its objective and was forced to retire under perilous machine-gun fire, Private Temple and two companions were surrounded by the enemy. His companions were wounded, but he bravely held off the enemy, after which he assisted both his companions to a first-aid station.

Navy Cross

The Navy Cross is the maritime equivalent of the Distinguished Service Cross for naval personnel. It was awarded to THOMAS HOLCOMB, major, Second Battalion Sixth Marine Regiment, U.S. Marine Corps, of New Castle Delaware. From August 1917 to January 1918, Major Holcomb commanded the Second Battalion, Sixth Marine Regiment, at the marine barracks in Quantico, Virginia, in preparation of overseas duty. From February 1918 to July 1918, following his appointment to lieutenant colonel on June 4, 1920, he served with the American Expeditionary Force in France. He commanded the Second Battalion from August 1918 and served as second in command of the Sixth Marine Regiment, taking part in the Aisne defensive (Château-Thierry), the Aisne-Marne offensive (Soissons), the Marbache sector, the St. Mihiel offensive, the Meuse-Argonne offensive (Champagne and Argonne Forest) and the march to the Rhine in Germany following the armistice. In recognition of his distinguished services in France, he was awarded the Navy Cross, as well as the Silver Star with three Oak Leaf Clusters, a Meritorious Service Citation by the commander in chief of the AEF, the Purple Heart and was three times cited in general orders of the Second Division, AEF. The French government conferred on him the Cross of the Legion of Honor and three times awarded him the Croix de Guerre with Palm.

DELAWARE MEDALS, DECORATIONS AND INSIGNIA OF WORLD WAR I (AND MORE)

The veterans who served were recognized with medals and ribbons. They were memorialized in bronze and marble throughout the state.

The Delaware Mexican Border Service Medal

The Delaware Mexican Border Service Medal was established to recognize and honor primarily the men of the First Regiment, Delaware National Guard, who served in the Punitive Expedition to Mexico during the period between July 19, 1916, and February 1917. The Delaware Mexican Border Service Medal has a circular bronze planchet. The obverse shows the

Delaware State seal, which is surrounded by a band that reads, "GREAT SEAL OF THE STATE OF DELAWARE -1793-1847-1907." The reverse side bears the words, "AWARDED TO _____ BY AN ACT OF GENERAL ASSEMBLY OF DELAWARE IN RECOGNITION OF MEXICAN BORDER SERVICE UNDER THE CALL OF THE PRESIDENT JUNE 18th 1916."

The medal hangs from a bicolor ribbon with dark blue on the left and golden yellow on the right. There is a brooch at the top of the device that suspends the ribbon. The brooch is a rectangle with a superimposed diamond centered amid the word MEX<>ICO. It surmounts two crossed rifles with only the stocks and muzzles visible beneath the diamond. The diamond contains a Delaware Blue Hen and three tiny chicks.

The Delaware Mexican Border Service Medal. *Courtesy Delaware Military Heritage and Education Foundation.*

The Delaware World War I Victory Medal

Following the earlier precedent of minting a medal for service on the Mexican Border, in 1919, the Delaware legislature authorized a World War I Victory Medal for its veterans. Ten thousand medals were minted as an appreciation by the people of the state of Delaware for the military service of its sons. The medals were made of sterling silver. They were designed and manufactured by the firm of Millard F.

The Delaware World War I Victory Medal. *Courtesy Delaware Military Heritage and Education Foundation.*

Davis, jewelers in Wilmington, Delaware. The medal is a silver planchet. The face of the medal depicts a narrow wreath connecting the broad arms of a cross to create a nearly circular shape, which contains the state coat of arms of Delaware surrounded by the inscription "WORLD WAR SERVICE" at the top and "DELAWARE" at the bottom of the design. It is surmounted by an American eagle with extended wings. The original medals probably had a lacquered finish to preserve their luster The obverse side of the medal contains the inscription: "AWARDED TO _____ BY ACT OF THE GENERAL ASSEMBLY OF THE STATE OF DELAWARE, 1919."

The medals were numbered below the 1919 date. A wreath motif surrounds this text. The Delaware Victory Medal was suspended from a rainbow ribbon very similar to the federal Victory Medal. Some medals bear a large star of finished silver mounted on the ribbon, measuring 0.7 inches. This signified that the named recipient was either lost in action or from disease. Delaware suffered 270 fatalities during the war (of about 10,000 who served). Delaware was one of only twelve states to issue a state victory medal for its World War I veterans.

Federal World War I Victory Medal

The World War I Victory Medal is a service medal of the United States military that was first created in 1919, designed by James Earle Fraser. The medal was originally intended to be created by an act of the United States Congress, however the bill authorizing the medal never passed, leaving the service departments to create the award through general orders. The U.S. Army published orders authorizing the World War I Victory Medal in April 1919, and the U.S. Navy followed in June of that same year. Known until 1947 simply as the "Victory Medal," the World War I Victory Medal was awarded to any member of the U.S. military who had served in the armed forces between April 6, 1917, and November 11, 1918, for any military service; November 12, 1918, and August 5, 1919, for service in European Russia; November 23, 1918, and April 1, 1920, for service with the American Expeditionary Force in Siberia.

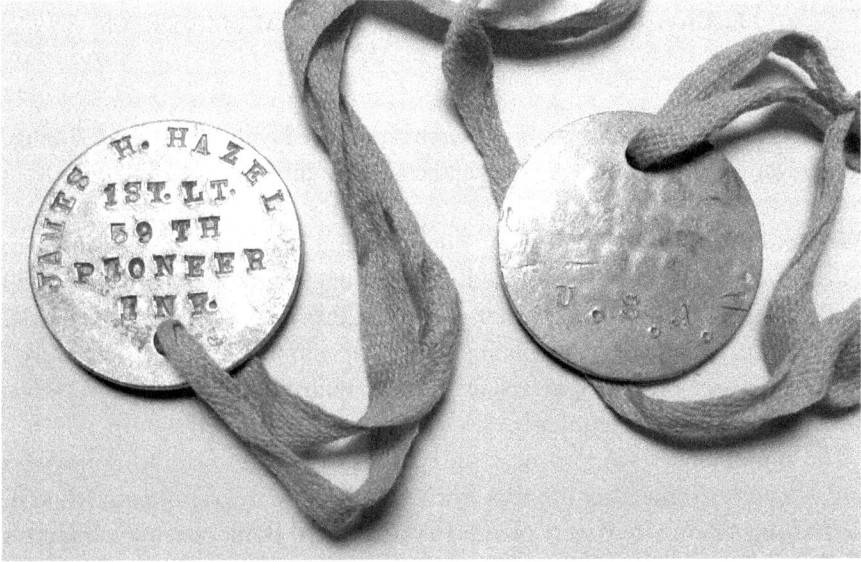

The dog tag identification disc for Lieutenant James H. Hazel of the Fifty-ninth Pioneer Infantry Regiment, Delaware National Guard. *Courtesy Delaware Military Heritage and Education Foundation.*

Dog Tags

The U.S. Army first authorized identification tags in War Department General Order, No. 204, dated December 20, 1906, which essentially prescribes the identification tag:

> *An aluminum identification tag, the size of a silver half dollar and of suitable thickness, stamped with the name, rank, company, regiment, or corps of the wearer, will be worn by each officer and enlisted man of the Army whenever the field kit is worn, the tag to be suspended from the neck, underneath the clothing, by a cord or thong passed through a small hole in the tab. It is prescribed as a part of the uniform and when not worn as directed herein will be habitually kept in the possession of the owner. The tag will be issued by the Quartermaster's Department gratuitously to enlisted men and at cost price to officers.*

The army changed regulations on July 6, 1916, so that all soldiers were issued two tags: one to stay with the body and the other to go to the person in charge of the burial for record-keeping purposes.

Delaware Monuments and Memorials of World War I

The Delaware veterans who served were recognized with medals and ribbons. They were memorialized in bronze and marble throughout the state.

Wilmington: The Washington Street Memorial Bridge, dedicated to Delaware's war dead, was opened in Wilmington after rebuilding in 1920 and formally dedicated on Memorial Day 1922 as the Washington Memorial Bridge. On the bridge are plaques with the names of all of Delaware's dead from previous wars, as well as some of their battles. Eagles and pylons provide architectural emphasis.

As in many places across the country, trees were planted for lost ones who did not come home after the war. Such was the case in Wilmington when in 1928 some twenty trees were planted along Bayard Boulevard (now Bancroft Parkway) in memory of departed heroes.

The Todd Memorial, also known as the Victory Monument, honors those who fought in World War I. It is located at Eighteenth Street and Baynard Boulevard. On Armistice Day, November 11, 1925, over nine thousand people gathered to see the memorial unveiled. Warm weather and cloudless skies ensured the good turnout for the ceremony. It is a thirty-five-foot bronze sculpture, paid for by local shipbuilder William H. Todd, with a figure of Winged Victory at the top. Augustus Lukeman created the sculpture. At the foot of the plaza, a granite base bears a bronze plaque listing the names of the Delawareans who died in the service of their county from 1917 to 1919. The granite plinth on which the bronze figure stands is carved with the words:

Erected in Honor of the
Soldiers and Sailors
of Delaware
Who Served in the World War
1917–1918
A Gift of William H. Todd
in Memory of His Father and Mother
1925

University of Delaware has a World War I marker near Old College, which is inscribed: "1917, 1918, In honor of the rural men of New Castle

County who entered the military service of their country on this spot during the First World War. This tablet is erected by the University of Delaware and the Community of Newark."

Memorial Hall, at the center of the campus, was conceived in 1918 at the end of the war as a living monument to "the memory of the men and women in this state who took part in the war." To emphasize that purpose, a book was compiled with each page containing the names and biographies of those Delawareans who died in the World War. The pages are on display in the atrium and turned daily by an ROTC student.

MIDDLETOWN: On November 11, 1919, town leaders in Middletown dedicated a monument at Four Corners, or Cochran Square, honoring four servicemen who died in World War I.

KIWANIS PARK, SEAFORD: The parks and recreation department unveiled a ten-foot-tall stone memorial in 1987 that lists the names of Seaford residents who died in World War I, World War II, Vietnam and Iraq. The park is on Stein Highway.

DELAWARE VETERANS CEMETERIES: The New Castle County cemetery is at 2465 Chesapeake City Road in Summit. The fifty-two-acre site is the final resting place for veterans of all wars since World War I. Fifteen markers represent the Delaware Medal of Honor recipients, although only one, James P. Connor, is buried there. The sixty-two-acre Sussex County Cemetery is at 26669 Patriots Way in Millsboro.

CODA: DOUGLAS MACARTHUR ON WORLD WAR I

In an address to the West Point Corps of Cadets in May 1962, General Douglas MacArthur recalled:

> *As I listened to those songs (of the West Point glee club) in memory's eye I could see those staggering columns of the First World War, bending under soggy packs, on many a weary march from dripping dusk to drizzling dawn, slogging ankle deep through the mire of shell shocked road, to form grimly for the attack, blue lipped, covered with sludge and mud, chilled by wind and rain, driving home to their objective, and for many, to the*

judgment of God. I do not know the dignity of their birth, but I do know the glory of their death. They died unquestioning, uncomplaining, with faith in their heart, and on their lips the hope that we would go on to victory. Always for them; Duty, Honor, Country; always their blood, sweat, and tears, as we sought the way and the light and the truth.

BIBLIOGRAPHY

Broyles, Randall L. *Concepts of Delaware*. West Palm Beach, FL: Universal Publishing Associates, 1974.

Bush, J. Danforth. *History of the 59th Pioneer Infantry, 1918–1919: American Expeditionary Forces*. Toul, France: Imprimerie LeMaire, 1919.

Delaware State Portrait Commission. *Catalog of Delaware State Portraits in the Capitol Buildings*. Dover, DE: 1941.

Devine, Donn. *The Delaware National Guard: A Historical Sketch*. Wilmington, DE: Adjutant General's Office, 1968.

Doerrfeld, Dean A., David L. Ames, Bernard L. Herman and Rebecca J. Siders. *The Delaware Ship and Boat Building Industry, 1830–1940: An Historic Context*. Newark, DE: Center for Historic Architecture and Engineering, College of Urban Affairs and Public Policy, University of Delaware, 1994.

Feuer, A.B. *The U.S. Navy in World War I*. Westport, CT: Praeger, 1999.

Frebert, George J. *Delaware Aviation History*. Dover, DE: Dover Litho Printing Company, 1998.

Gorrell, Edgar S. "Histories of the Sixteenth, Seventeenth, Nineteenth and Twentieth Aero Squadrons." In *History of the American Expeditionary Forces Air Service, 1917–1919*. Series E, Vol. 4. Washington, D.C.: National Archives, 1974.

Harris, Charles H., III, and Louis R. Sadler. *The Great Call-Up*. Norman: University of Oklahoma Press, 2015.

Hickey, Joseph P. "Race and War in Delaware: The Story of Delaware's African American Veterans of World War I." Synthesis, University of Delaware, 2005.

Huber, Harold. *With Eyes of Faith: A History of Greenwood Mennonite Church, Greenwood, Delaware, 1914–1974*. Greenwood, DE: Country Rest Home, 1974.

Ianni, Francis A. *World War One Remembered*. Wilmington: Delaware Heritage Press, 1993.

Jones, Jerry W. *United States Battleship Operations in World War One.* Annapolis, MD: Naval Institute Press, 1998.

Leeke, Jim. "The Delaware River Shipbuilding League, 1918." *National Pastime: From Swampoodle to South Philly; Baseball in Philadelphia and the Delaware Valley*, July 2013.

Lincoln, Anna T., Leslie Carpenter and Georg H. Ryden. *Highlights of Wilmington Delaware, 1832–1932, Commemorating the 100th Anniversary of the Granting of the Corporate Charter to the Borough of Wilmington by the Delaware State Legislature.* Wilmington, DE: Charter Centennial Celebration, 1932.

Manthorpe, William H.J., Jr. *A Century of Service: The U.S. Navy on Cape Henlopen, Lewes, Delaware, 1898–1996.* Wilmington, DE: Cedar Tree Press, 2014.

Martin, Roger A. *A History of Delaware through Its Governors, 1774–1984.* Wilmington, DE: McClafferty Press, 1984.

———. *Tales of Delaware.* Wilmington, DE, 1991.

Massie, Robert K. *Castles of Steel: Britain, Germany, and the Winning of the Great War at Sea.* New York: Random House, 2003.

———. *Dreadnought.* New York: Random House, 1991.

Maurer, Maurer, ed. *The US Air Service in World War I.* Washington, D.C.: Office of Air Force History, 1978.

McNinch, Marjorie G. *Wilmington in Vintage Postcards.* Charleston, SC: Arcadia Publishing, 2000.

Molek, Mary, ed. *I Remember When: The World War Periods at Home and Abroad; A Treasury of Reminiscences.* Newark: University of Delaware Continuing Education, 1981.

Monroe, John A. *History of Delaware.* Newark: University of Delaware Press, 1979.

Navy Department. Office of the Chief of Naval Operations. Division of Naval History. "History of Ships Named Delaware." Ship's Histories, Historical Society of Delaware, 1960.

Tyler, D.B., *The American Clyde: A History of Iron and Steel Shipbuilding on the Delaware from 1840 to World War I.* Newark: University of Delaware Press, 1958.

War Department. U.S. Adjutant General's Office. *Congressional Medal of Honor, the Distinguished Service Cross and the Distinguished Service Medal Issued by the War Department Since April 6, 1917: Up to and Including General Orders, No. 126.* Washington, D.C., November 11, 1919.

Warrington, C.W. *Delaware's Coastal Defenses.* Wilmington: Delaware Heritage Press, 2003.

Wiggins, Kennard R., Jr. *Delaware Army National Guard.* Charleston, SC: Arcadia Publishing, 2010.

Wilson, W. Emerson. *Fort Delaware.* Newark: University of Delaware Press, 1957.

Wysock, Rolf J. *One Hundred Years of Military Science at the University of Delaware.* Newark: University of Delaware, 1989.

INDEX

ABOUT THE AUTHOR

Kennard Wiggins is a retired Delaware Air National Guard officer. He writes about his native state of Delaware, mostly on historical military topics. Wiggins serves as the vice-chairman of the Delaware Military Heritage and Education Foundation. He is the president of the board of trustees for the Cecil County Public Library system and vice-chairman of the Cecil County Planning Commission.

Kennard Wiggins is also the author of *Delaware Air National Guard, Delaware Army National Guard* and *Dover Air Force Base*; co-author of *Delaware Aviation*; and contributing author to *Histories of Newark, 1758–2008*.

www.ingramcontent.com/pod-product-compliance
Lightning Source LLC
Chambersburg PA
CBHW060802100426
42813CB00004B/914

*9 7 8 1 5 4 0 2 1 4 0 4 1 *